MILLER'S
FIELD GUIDE
PORCELAIN

Consultant: Gordon Lang
Series Editor: Judith Miller

MILLER'S

Miller's Field Guide: Porcelain
Consultant: Gordon Lang

Miller's, a division of Mitchell Beazley,
both imprints of Octopus Publishing Group Ltd
Endeavour House, 189 Shaftesbury Avenue, London WC2H 8JY
www.octopusbooks.co.uk
www.octopusbooksusa.com
Miller's is a registered trademark of Octopus Publishing Group Ltd.

Series Editor:	Judith Miller
Publisher:	Alison Starling
Chief Contributors:	Judith Miller and Steven Moore
Editorial Co-ordinator:	Christina Webb
Editorial Assistant:	Fiona Eccles
Proofreader:	Jo Murray
Indexer:	Diana LeCore
Art Director:	Jonathan Christie
Designer:	Ali Scrivens, T J Graphics
Production Controller:	Sarah Connelly

Copyright © Octopus Publishing Group Ltd 2014

Some of the text in this edition was originally published in *Miller's Antiques Checklist: Porcelain* in
1991, reprinted 1994, 1995, 1996, 1997, 1998, 1999, 2000.

Distributed in the US by	Distributed in Canada by
Hachette Book Group	Canadian Manda Group
1290 Avenue of the Americas	664 Annette St.
4th and 5th Floors	Toronto, Ontario, Canada M6S 2C8
New York, NY 10020	

ISBN 978 1 84533 949 4

The publishers will be grateful for any information that will assist them in keeping further editions
up to date. Although all reasonable care has been taken in the preparation of this book, neither the
publishers nor the compilers accept any liability for any consequences arising from the use thereof,
nor the information contained herein.

A CIP catalogue record for this book is available from the British Library

Set in Chronicle Deck, Roman, Semi Italic and Bold
Printed and bound in China

A Flight, Barr & Barr Worcester pot-pourri vase. c. 1815–20
12.2in (30.5cm) high E

Contents

*A Vienna "Veduti"
cup. 1846
4in (10cm) high E*

*An 18thC Ludwigsburg soup tureen and
cover, damaged.
14in (35.5cm) high G*

A Meissen figure, modelled by Kändler and Reinicke. c.1755 6.75in (17cm) high E

A Worcester famille verte *teapot. c.1752–5 5in (12.5cm) high E*

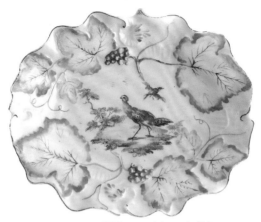

A Longton Hall dish. c.1755 8in (20.5cm) wide E

VALUE CODES

Throughout this book the value codes used at the end of each caption correspond to the approximate value of the item. These are broad price ranges and should only be seen as a guide, as prices for antiques vary depending on the condition of the item, geographical location, and market trends. The codes used are as follows:

AAA £100,000+ ($170,000+)

AA £50,000–100,000 ($85,000-170,000)

A £25,000–50,000 ($40,000–85,000)

B £15,000–25,000 ($25,000–40,000)

C £10,000–15,000 ($17,000–25,000)

D £5,000–10,000 ($8,500–17,000)

E £2,000–5,000 ($3,500–8,500)

F £1,000–2,000 ($2,000–3,500)

G £500–1,000 ($850–2,000)

H under £500 (under $850)

Collecting porcelain

The practice of collecting porcelain in a systematic manner is probably a relatively late phenomenon in the Western world, although various pieces are included in the inventories of great and noble families in France and Italy during the 14thC and 15thC – for example, a shallow porcelain bowl is recorded among the treasures of Louis, Duke of Anjou in 1379–80, probably as it was rare and costly rather than as part of a formal collection. Almost certainly not until the 17thC, when porcelain was available in far greater quantities than ever, especially in Europe, could anything resembling a system or classification be applied to the collecting of porcelain. However, it was an enthusiasm that caught on quickly: the early 18thC English novelist and essayist Daniel Defoe referred to what he once regarded as Queen Mary's excessive mania for collecting china. Since then, collectors have become increasingly sophisticated in their approach to porcelain collecting, especially in the last generations or so.

Within the same space of 20 years, an enormous number of specialized books, monographs, and papers have helped to illuminate this vast topic. Ongoing excavations and research force constant reappraisal, especially with regard to attribution. In the 1960s attributions were generally looser – for example, the terms "Rockingham" and "Coalport" were freely applied to anything encrusted

A Meissen Böttger porcelain beaker, with silver mount. c.1715–20 6in (15cm) high D

8

A Rockingham encrusted porcelain pot-pourri basket and cover. c.1830–42 3.25in (8cm) diam H

with flowers or even Neo-rococo in style. The same was true of many porcelains then classified as "Liverpool" but which in the light of recent research have today been identified as Vauxhall or Limehouse. However, although it is possible to be fairly precise in attributing most porcelain, there are still many under-researched areas in which an astute and assiduous amateur could discover pieces of interest at undervalued prices. Whether you are buying porcelain for its decorative appeal or its rarity, or even for its association with a historical person or event, the choice is very broad. Some collectors concentrate on a specific factory, period, type of object, or decorative theme. It is essential to gain as much experience as possible from handling and examining pieces known to be genuine. Time spent at museums to become familiar with the best examples is a good foundation, but it is equally, if not more important to actually handle the porcelain pieces themselves. The best places to do this are the auction houses and stores of specialist dealers. Bear in mind that the more research you have done, and the more interest you manifest, the more experts will be inclined to discuss their subject and their stock.

Marks

Although many people look for a mark first as a way of identifying a piece of porcelain, marks can be deceptive – for example, a good number of factories copied the marks of more fashionable porcelains, especially those of Meissen

A Vauxhall mug. c.1757 3.75in (9.5cm) high F

of spectacular exceptions such as Capodimonte (see pp.116–117) and Nymphenburg (see pp.66–7). However, buying what is unfashionable now may well prove in time to have been a good investment. Rare examples of any type of porcelain will always command high prices, whereas in other cases more mundane specimens are subject to greater fluctuations in the market. Condition is very important: while rare or important pieces that are no longer in perfect condition still command enormous sums, the damaged run-of-the-mill porcelain finds should be avoided, except perhaps as study pieces.

and Sèvres. Therefore, more emphasis has been placed in this book on teaching collectors how to identify a piece through other, more reliable signs, such as the paste, the type of glaze, the style of the piece, and so on. The mark should then be used merely as confirmation of what has already been deduced by looking at these other "clues".

The market

Potential buyers should find out what is currently enjoying a boom and what is in the doldrums. At the moment there is generally greater interest in wares than in figures, although there are a number

This book

The method used throughout this book is founded in the visual analysis of porcelain, it is the same systematic procedure as that employed by a forensic scientist looking for clues, and therefore it, too, requires the same patience and also the power of observation. The book concentrates on the work of all the important kiln sites and European and American porcelains, and in each case on the period or wares of greatest interest to collectors: even some of the major factories would sometimes produce wares that are not

10

A late 19thC Samson box and cover, in the Meissen style. G

highly collectable.

A special section at the back of the book also looks at copies and fakes and distinguishes between copies that have over time become collectable in their own right and out-and-out frauds. However, remember that making mistakes is all part of the learning process – even top dealers have sometimes been fooled. With time, you will acquire the experience and confidence to make informed and sound judgements and with that will come the joy and satisfaction of collecting porcelain.

A late 19thC Sèvres porcelain and gilt-metal covered vase. 22.5in (57cm) high E

How to look at porcelain

Paste

The first step in identifying a piece of porcelain is to examine the paste, that is, the unglazed porcelain body, which can usually be seen on the base. The only time when this is not possible is when the piece has been glazed overall,

A late 18thC Doccia model of a young woman. 5.5in (14cm) high F

A Meissen Marcolini period blanc de Chine *porcelain figure. c.1800 24in (61cm) high F*

like the Bow flatwares, which stood on tiny stilts in the kiln. But on these rare occasions the overall glaze is itself a clue to the piece's identity. The first question to ask when examining a piece is whether the paste looks like sand or like icing (confectioner's) sugar. In other words, is it granular, or smooth, or some stage in between? If it tends towards the granular, it is more likely to be soft-paste; if it tends towards the smooth, it is more likely to be hard-paste. There are of course exceptions, which can only

A Meissen pagoda figure. c.1730
4in (10cm) high C

in Europe at Meissen, in Saxony, at the beginning of the 18thC. The essential ingredients are two types of decomposed granite, kaolin (china clay) and petuntse (china stone), which fuse to the hard consistency of glass in the high temperatures of the kiln. Having decided whether the porcelain is hard- or soft-paste, there is one last question to be asked about the paste. Can the factory be identified by the colour? For example, is the paste pure white, like *blanc de Chine*, is it a dark colour, like the grey paste of Doccia, or has oxidization in the firing stained it with tiny brown patches, like Lowestoft?

be learned with experience, and there are also some pieces that are deceptive. For example, the bases on some Chelsea wares are ground away, which makes the unglazed areas look very smooth, although in fact the porcelain is a granular soft-paste.

Soft-paste was developed in Italy under the patronage of the Medicis at the end of the 16thC. It scratches and chips more easily than hard-paste, and the chips, which look like broken biscuit, are very different from the smooth hard-paste chips.

Hard-paste is the formula for Chinese porcelain, which was first made

A First Period Worcester tankard, painted in the "Prunus Fence" pattern. c.1755–60
6in (15.5cm) high G

A Chelsea plate, in Meissen style, red anchor mark. c.1758 8in (20.5cm) diam F

Glaze

In studying the glaze, we are also looking at different stages between extremes: is it either dull or matt on the one hand, or alternatively, smooth or glassy? Is it transparent or is it opaque? Is it thick or thin? The glaze can be as much a clue to a piece's origin as the paste. For example, Mennecy and Saint-Cloud used a glaze that was very transparent, while Doccia and Chantilly used an opaque glaze with tin in the formula, probably in order to hide blemishes in the paste. On early Worcester the glaze is very thin, while on gold-anchor Chelsea it is exceptionally thick. In general the glazes on soft-pastes are thick and tend to conceal the details. As a result, soft-paste figures often look like melting ice and suffer in comparison with thin-glazed, hard-paste examples.

If a glaze contracts more than the paste as it cools down after firing, it breaks into a network of irregular cracks, known as crackle. As this tended to happen at some factories more than at others, it can be another clue to the identity of a piece. For example, it is found on the thick-glazed, gold-anchor Chelsea wares and on several other

A pair of Sèvres sauce tureens and covers, painted by Nicolas Bulidon. 1771 9in (23cm) long D

A Bloor Derby porcelain "Earl Spencer's House" topographical vase. c.1820 11.5in (29cm) high F

usually to examine the colours. Most factories used different palettes. For example, in the Meissen Kakiemon palette, the prominent colours are a greyish turquoise, sky blue and iron red; and lemon yellow, purple, and gold. But at other factories different colours dominate, and in the original Japanese palette the turquoise is more vibrant and translucent, the yellow is dirty, and there is no purple. Some factories use more gilding than others. The next step is to study the subject and determine whether it is Oriental or European. The subject itself can mean nothing: many Chinese export wares were decorated with European soft-pastes, and also on early Chinese stoneware, where it was often produced to obtain a decorative effect.

Decoration

The style and technique of the decoration are often important evidence of a piece's origin. Decoration can be incised or moulded, printed or painted; and it can be applied over the glaze, which can usually be felt with the fingers. But the most useful first step is

A pair of late 19thC Berlin urns. 25in (66.5cm) high A

A mid-18thC Höchst teapot and cover.
6in (15.5cm) high F

A Meissen group of figures, by J. J. Kändler.
c.1740 8in (20.5cm) long D

Dating

The Chinese potters were very conservative. It could take a hundred years to change a pattern. Some of their designs lasted for several centuries. As a result, it is often difficult to date Chinese wares by their decoration, but European factories were always subject to changing fashions. The style of a piece often gives a good indication of its date. In the early 18thC, designs were balanced and tightly organized. Even the wild chinoiseries of J. G. Herold at Meissen were governed by a desire for symmetry. In the late 1740s the Rococo style began to replace the Baroque. Brown and puce crept into the palettes. Designs became livelier and there was an increased use of gilding. By the mid-1750s the French royal factory at Sèvres had replaced Meissen as the leader of fashion. Under its influence, figures became more exuberant with swirling, scrolled bases, and in England they were built up with bright backdrops of applied flowers. However, it was also in France that the more disciplined Neo-classical style began to appear in the late 1750s. Shapes became rectilinear and followed the forms of Classical bronzes. Bright ground colours were replaced with sepias and greys. Festoons and garlands surrounded designs in small oval and

scenes, and many of the finest European porcelains are decorated with Oriental designs. But the artists on each continent have never represented one another entirely convincingly.

A pair of late 18thC Chelsea porcelain bocage *groups. 10.5in (26.5cm) high G*

octagonal reserves.

At the end of the 18thC, the second phase of Neo-classicism, which included the French empire style, was much more self-important and sumptuous. Gilt, dark ground colours, and rich grandiose decorations covered all the porcelain. Vases and other decorative pieces were often mounted on elaborate, gilded bronze stands. But by this time there was little individuality. The styles of the leading factories had become so similar that today it is often difficult to tell them apart. During the last years of Neo-classicism, especially in England, a pretentious Neo-rococo style emerged. Then came the Gothic revival, and after the Great Exhibition of 1851 the English factories produced scores of similar pastiches of almost every earlier style. The shape can also reveal a great deal about a piece of porcelain. Before the European potters developed their own shapes under the influence of the prevailing fashions, they drew their inspiration from other materials and other traditions. The Rococo and Neo-

But there are other ways in which the maker of a model can be identified. The first step is to find out how the figure was made (provided that the base is not covered over). There are basically two methods. In the first method,

An 18thC Derby porcelain figure of a shepherdess. 5.75in (14.5cm) high H

classical styles had their own shapes as well as decorations, but the earlier European wares followed the shapes of silverware and pottery or else copied the Oriental forms.

Figures

The styles of the individual porcelain modellers are as unique as their signatures, and the works of the greatest artists are often easily recognizable.

A Höchst figure of a girl. c.1760 6.25in (16cm) high H

known as slipcasting, the liquid clay, or slip, is poured into an absorbent mould made of earthenware or plaster of Paris. After a few hours, the mould has absorbed the liquid and a layer of clay has built up inside it to form the figure. Slipcast figures are light and have smooth interiors, which, where not covered over, show all the shapes of the exteriors. The second method, press moulding, is a more skilful operation, in which the moulder has to press the wet clay into the mould with his fingers. Figures made in this way are much heavier. They have thumb prints and an irregular surface on the interior; and light shows through where the paste is thinnest. Most Continental figures, except those made at Meissen pre-1763 and Tournai pre-1784, are slipcast, as are all English figures except those of Bow, Plymouth, Bristol, and Worcester. Most Oriental figures before c.1800 are press-moulded. Many press-moulded pieces were made in two parts and then joined together, and it is often possible to detect the seam. The bases are also very important for identification: the style can narrow the field to a small group or even a single factory. Similarly, base decorations can be a clue. At the height of the Rococo, many Frankenthal bases were covered with moss, while their Meissen equivalents were covered with flowers.

Idiosyncrasies

Many factories have individual characteristics that make their wares easy to identify. For example, a lot of

A Chelsea figure of a shepherdess, with gold anchor mark. c.1760 5.5in (14cm) high F

19

A pair of late 19thC Samson models of lovers, after Derby. 12.5in (32cm) high H

Bow wares are heavily potted and do not allow the light to pass through, while other wares, such as Chelsea's, are highly translucent. Chelsea in particular has an unusual characteristic in that certain patches, known as moons, look brighter and allow much more light to pass through than the rest of the body. Other idiosyncrasies include methods of firing. For example, Chelsea dishes were fired on stilts, which left three blemishes protruding from the underside. Derby wares were fired on a tripod of pads, whereas Chinese

Dingyao and Qingbai porcelains were fired on their mouthrims, which left them unglazed.

Condition

Some collectors prefer a piece to be restored rather than left in a damaged state, but usually restoration reduces the value. If a piece has been chipped, or if it has a broken section that has been glued back on, it will usually be worth a lot more than a piece with so much over-painting that it is difficult to assess the extent of the original damage.

Marks

It is important for every collector to own a good book of marks. We have recently published *Miller's Antiques Marks*, which covers not only ceramics, but also silver, sculpture, glass, costume jewellery, dolls, teddies, and toys. However, it is also important to regard all marks with extreme caution. Most of them reveal very little. The vast majority of Meissen and Sèvres marks are spurious. For example, after the French Revolution a large number of white Sèvres pieces were sold off to decorators who painted them in their own workshops and marked them with interlaced "L"s in order to pass them off as the real thing. Because of the success of Meissen, the crossed swords mark was often used by other factories in Dresden but also by factories across Europe. It was often used on soft-paste porcelain in France and England. Similarly, most Chinese reign marks are equally misleading: Chinese potters inscribed their wares with the marks of earlier reigns out of respect for the artistry of their predecessors; and, for less honourable reasons, many Japanese potters put reign marks on their products in order to pass them off as Chinese. Individual potters rarely had their own mark. Since it is seldom reliable, the mark is the last thing to look at when attempting to identify a piece of porcelain. The most important help to identifying and dating porcelain is to examine authentic pieces in auction rooms and in specialist antique dealers' shops. It is also invaluable to go to ceramic galleries in museums. Make sure to look at one factory at a time, and, as we have done in this book, interrogate the piece in order to find its unique porcelain DNA.

A Sèvres bowl, cover, and stand. 1785
6.25in (16cm) diam E

This Sèvres mark 1785

Porcelain colours

The colours, or enamels, used to decorate porcelain often provide an important clue to the date or origin of a piece. Some factories used such distinctive palettes that a

Turquoise
(Meissen, Derby, c.1770)

Bleu Celeste
(Sèvres)

Turquoise
(Chelsea, 1760s)

Emerald Green
(Bow)

Apple Green
(Worcester, Sèvres)

Böttger Green
(Early Meissen)

Brunswick Green
(English factories)

Lemon Yellow
(Meissen c.1730–50)

Tan
(German and Swiss factories)

single dominant colour can be enough to identify their wares. In the same way, the wrong colour can give away an otherwise convincing fake. It would be impossible to chart all the colours and tones ever used, but these two pages show the most common colours and identify the eras when they were fashionable and the manufacturers who introduced them or used them most often.

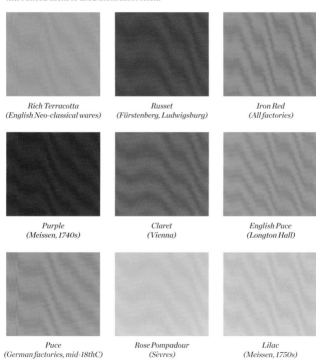

Rich Terracotta
(English Neo-classical wares)

Russet
(Fürstenberg, Ludwigsburg)

Iron Red
(All factories)

Purple
(Meissen, 1740s)

Claret
(Vienna)

English Puce
(Longton Hall)

Puce
(German factories, mid-18thC)

Rose Pompadour
(Sèvres)

Lilac
(Meissen, 1750s)

European porcelain

For a thousand years after its discovery, porcelain was a mystery in Europe. In the 13thC the traveller Marco Polo described the beautiful porcelain bowls of Fujian; and in the 14thC and 15thC a few individual pieces were itemized in aristocratic inventories. However, the Europeans did not attempt to make porcelain themselves until late in the 16thC, after the Portuguese had begun to import it in substantial quantities.

A Sèvres saucer, with a nude Classical maiden.
1784 5.5in (14cm) diam E

In 1575, Duke Francesco de Medici opened a porcelain factory in Florence. In France, almost a hundred years later, the Poterat family founded a factory in Rouen, and a few years after that a second French factory was established at Saint-Cloud near Paris. In England, as early as 1671, John Dwight of Fulham took out a patent on a porcelain formula, although there is no evidence that he ever made any. But all these porcelains were hybrid soft-pastes. It was not until 1708 that the alchemist Johann Friedrich Böttger produced the first European formula for a true hard-paste porcelain. In the following year, his patron, Augustus the Strong, Elector of Saxony, opened a factory at Meissen.

A Chantilly box and cover. c.1740–50
2.5in (6.5cm) long F

A Meissen tea caddy and cover, decorated by Johann Ehrenfried Stadler. c.1728 4in (10cm) high D

*An early Meissen saucer, painted in the
manner of Aufenwerth. c.1730
5in (12.5cm) diam G*

Meissen's once secret formula began
to spread across Europe as greedy
employees sought quick profit.
Goldsmith Conrad Hunger obtained the
formula and set out with Samuel Stölzel
for Vienna and established a factory
with Claudius du Paquier. Another
Meissen employee, Adam Friedrich von
Löwenfink, established Höchst. Soon
afterwards three Höchst employees

went to Fürstenberg under
the Duke of Brunswick.
By 1770, there were
almost 20 hard-paste
factories in Europe.
The first Italian
hard-paste factory
was founded
in Venice by
goldsmith
Francesco Vezzi,
c.1720, with the
help of Conrad
Hunger. The
factory closed
c.1727, when
Hunger returned to
Meissen, cutting off
the supply of clay from
Saxony. In 1735 Doccia was
established near Florence and
in 1764 another Venetian factory
was founded by Geminiano Cozzi.
The well known Capodimonte factory
was established in 1743 near Naples.
In France, soft-paste continued in
production for most of the 18thC.
Following Rouen and Saint-Cloud, the
Prince of Condé established a factory
at Chantilly and the Duc de Villeroy
opened one in Paris, which later moved
to Mennecy. In 1756 the 18-year-old
factory at Vincennes moved to Sèvres,
later to be owned by King Louis XV.
Protected by sumptuary laws, which

among other things prevented other factories from using gilding, the French royal factory prospered. After the Seven Years' War, which ended in 1763, Sèvres took over from Meissen as the leader in European fashion. Five years later the factory acquired a hard-paste formula, and from then until the Revolution, while hard-paste gradually replaced soft-paste, it made magnificent, coloured-ground wares embellished with the finest gilding ever seen on porcelain. Although several hard-paste factories sprang up around Paris after the Revolution, none of them was a match for Sèvres, and for all their quality, their wares differed little in style from the products of Meissen, Berlin, or Vienna. England came comparatively late to the manufacture of porcelain. Chelsea, Bow, and Lund's of Bristol did not begin production until the 1740s, soon followed by Derby, Longton Hall, Lowestoft,

and the first hard-paste factory, Plymouth. Apart from Worcester, Lowestoft, and Derby, these factories were short-lived affairs or were taken over by larger concerns. Worcester was the most successful of the 18thC English porcelain factories. The body was finely potted with a thin glaze. Richard Chaffers's Liverpool factory mostly used blue and white decoration although some wares used the *famille rose* palette.

A Longton Hall saucer dish, painted by the "Castle" painter. c.1755 8in (20.5cm) diam E

Porcelain centres

Porcelain has to combine durability with delicateness. It has to be practical and it also has to be attractive. It has captivated people since the first pieces reached the West from China during the Dark Ages. No one is exactly sure when porcelain was discovered but probably somewhere in China a naturally occurring fine white clay must have contained both kaolin and petuntse (felspar). Kaolin, known as china clay, is a form of decomposed granite and is 98 per cent kaolinite. When fired at a high temperature it would fuse into a special kind of white pottery that could be transparent. Porcelain, the "white gold" was born.

There followed centuries of European travellers coming back with examples of this wonderful material. Emperors and kings vied to discover the secret of this miraculous substance. Initial porcelain made in Italy and France was soft-paste or "artificial". Accounts of a fine white clay contained in rocks mined near Colditz came to the attention of an alchemist called Johann Friedrich Böttger who had been imprisoned by Augustus the Strong in his castle in Dresden in Saxony. The clay was, of course, kaolin. Meissen went to enormous lengths to prevent other factories discovering the secret but soon many factories sprang up in Germany and beyond, making hard-paste porcelain. In England, France, and Italy soft-paste porcelain was made that doesn't contain kaolin. What is interesting about the English factories is that they tended to be private enterprises, unlike the royal-sponsored factories in Germany and France. As they were mainly producing soft-paste porcelain, many of them struggled to make a profit. Chelsea made a glassy frit body, while Bow added animal bone. Probably the most successful factory, Worcester, added a secret ingredient "soaprock", which was a steatite mined in Cornwall. Although not as sophisticated as the hard-paste of Meissen, it gave Worcester's soft-paste remarkable strength. Many English factories used burnt animal bones to make bone china. Bone china was 50 per cent bone combined with equal measures of quartz and felspar. It was strong, very white, and translucent. Josiah Spode is usually credited with its invention in c.1800. It is essential to handle as much porcelain as possible to determine firstly whether it is hard- or soft-paste, and then where and when it was made.

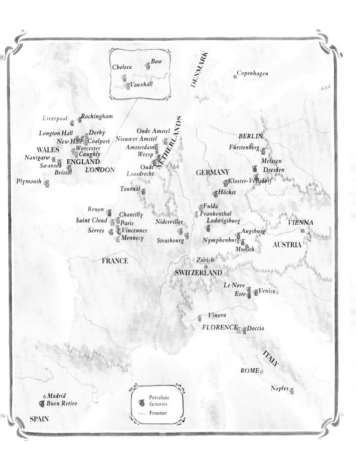

Chelsea Bow
Vauxhall

Copenhagen

DENMARK

Liverpool Rockingham
Longton Hall Derby
New Hall Coalport
WALES Worcester Caughly
Nantgarw ENGLAND
Swansea LONDON
Bristol
Plymouth

Oude Amstel
Nieuwer Amstel
Amsterdam
Weesp
Oude
Loosdrecht

NETHERLANDS

BERLIN
Fürstenberg

Meissen
Dresden

GERMANY
Kloster-Veilsdorf
Höchst

Tournai

Rouen
Saint Cloud Chantilly
Paris
Sèvres Vincennes
Mennecy

Niderviller

Strasbourg

Fulda
Frankenthal
Ludwigsburg

Augsburg
Nymphenburg
Munich

VIENNA

AUSTRIA

FRANCE

Zürich
SWITZERLAND

Le Nove
Este Venice

Vinovo
FLORENCE Doccia

ITALY

ROME

Naples

Madrid
Buen Retiro

SPAIN

Porcelain
factories
Frontier

29

Early Meissen

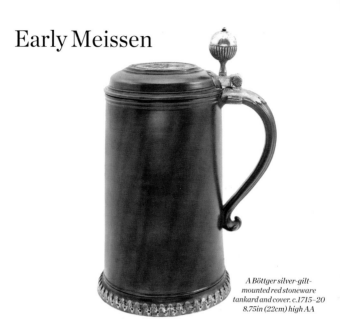

A Böttger silver-gilt-mounted red stoneware tankard and cover. c.1715–20 8.75in (22cm) high AA

1. If the piece is stoneware, is it very close-grained?
2. Has the piece been polished or cut into facets?
3. Is there carved decoration?
4. Is the piece the shape of silverware?
5. If the piece is porcelain, is it hard-paste?
6. Is the glaze warm and creamy?
7. Are there any splits or tears where the paste has dried out too soon?

Europe's first hard-paste porcelain

In Saxony, in the late 17thC, an amateur scientist, Count von Tschirnhaus, tried to find a formula for hard-paste porcelain. After years of failure, his luck changed in 1707 when he acquired the unwilling assistance of Prussian alchemist, Johann Friedrich Böttger.

Johann Friedrich Böttger (1682–1719)

Böttger had such a great reputation in Prussia that many people, including King Frederick I, believed he was close to discovering a formula for gold. Fearing rightly that the impercunious king was planning to lock him up until he succeeded, Böttger fled to Saxony, where he was seized for the same purposes by Augustus the Strong. Augustus kept Böttger under guard and forced him to continue his experiments. In 1707, frustrated by their inevitable failure, he ordered him to stop and assist

A rare Meissen Böttger porcelain fluted bowl and cover. c.1720 6in (15.5cm) high D

Tschirnhaus instead. In 1710 Augustus the Strong set up the Royal Saxon Porcelain Factory in his castle at Meissen, near Dresden, where Böttger was being held. The factory produced luxury wares based on shapes used on contemporary silver. On 15 January 1708, Böttger and Tschirnhaus recorded a formula for porcelain, which proved successful in the first firing. Böttger also built kilns that could produce the high temperatures required. In 1710 the new factory began to produce its famous red stoneware, and in 1713 it exhibited Europe's first hard-paste porcelain. In 1714 Böttger was appointed administrator of the factory and finally granted his freedom. On 13 March 1719, he died at the age of 37 an alcoholic.

A Böttger pagoda figure and incense burner. c.1720 2.5in (6.5cm) high D

Meissen porcelain 1720s

*A Meissen Böttger
teapot. c.1723 5.5in
(14cm) high D*

1. Is the porcelain hard-paste?
2. Is it close-grained, greyish, and a little chalky?
3. If the base is flat, are there little flecks on the unglazed surface?
4. Are puce and iron red dominant in the decoration?
5. If there are figures, are they standing on a surface of milky green?
6. If the piece is in the Kakiemon style, are the enamels sunk into
    the porcelain?
7. Do figures depict Orientals or merchants?

Johann Gregor Herold (1696–1775)

In 1720 Johann Gregor Herold arrived from Vienna. He succeeded Böttger as administrator and in 1723 he was appointed court painter. Under Herold, Meissen acquired the decorations and palette that were to make it famous.

Chinoiserie

Based on earlier prints, Herold designed tranquil Oriental scenes.

• Figures are elongated, like figures in fashion plates.

• They stand on terraces supported by gilded Baroque scrollwork and frames.

• Scenes painted before 1725 generally have clouds in the background.

Early palette

Herold's early designs are dominated by iron red and puce. This style was copied by other factories, but the colour that distinguishes Meissen is the rich milky green beneath the figures. Within the scrollwork, there is also a pinkish lustre. From 1729 copies of Kakiemon wares were produced. These copies, which were intended to be as close as possible to the originals, have noticeable differences:

• The Japanese painting is looser.

• The enamels on Meissen wares have sunk in and lie flush with the surface of the porcelain. On real Kakiemon wares, the enamels lie proud.

• In addition, there is a type of Meissen flower painting that is a mixture

Meissen vases. c.1730 2.5in (6.5cm) high D

of Japanese Kakiemon and Chinese *famille verte*.

Herold was a brilliant colourist, fine painter, and designer. In the late 1720s he introduced a series of solid coloured grounds with a flawless surface. The most popular of these colours were:

• turquoise

• imperial, egg-yolk yellow

• pea green

• strong sea green

• puce or claret

• tomato red.

Hard-paste porcelain

Meissen's early hard-paste has a warm, milky glaze. Designs were based on stoneware models.

Vessels often have moulded acanthus leaves around the base. Meissen was heavily influenced by Japan and China.

Marks

There are no identification marks on the earliest Meissen.

Meissen 1730s–40s

A Meissen chocolate pot and cover, decorated with a harbour scene. c.1745 D

1. Is decoration European in subject?
2. Is the glaze glassy, with "cold" blue look?
3. Are the handles wishbone-shaped?
4. Is the paste close-grained, slightly grey, and chalky?
5. Are scenes enclosed in lavish Rococo frames?

A Meissen teabowl, c.1735–40 3in (7.5cm) F

European decoration

During the 1730s, European themes became more popular than the Oriental pattern. Many of the wares from this period are decorated with harbour scenes (as on the chocolate pot, see left) or landscapes in the manner of painters such as Watteau and Lancret.

The new formula

After 1725, Meissen porcelain differs from the porous variety invented by Böttger. The paste is close-grained, slightly grey, and a little chalky; and there are extraneous slivers of clay sticking to the underside of pieces with flat unglazed bases. In addition, the

*A Meissen teapot and cover. c.1735
7in (18cm) high E*

glaze is much smoother and glassier, and has the cold, bluish look associated with the factory.

Identification points

- The handles on large vessels are wishbone-shaped with small scrolls at the joints.
- Handles on cups are simple loops with projections at the bottom.
- Pot lids are artichoke-shaped.

*A Meissen chinoiserie tea caddy. c.1730
4.5in (11.5cm) high E*

Marks

- Rare marks found on some wares after 1724 are the initials "KPM" (Königliche Porzellan Manufaktur).
- After 1725 the most common mark is the crossed swords in underglaze blue, from the arms of Saxony. From 1730 onwards, the angle between the swords becomes noticeably more acute.
- From c.1740 onwards, the mark is smaller – on most pieces it is less than ¾in (2cm) long.

Meissen 1770s–90s

A Meissen porcelain platter. c.1780 14in (35.5cm) wide D

1. Is the paste smooth, slightly off-white, and free from flecks?
2. Is the glaze glassier and somewhat bluer than earlier examples?
3. Are the colours even pales and more washed out than Rococo colours?
4. If the piece is a figure, does it have a slightly concave, glazed base?
5. Is the base of the figure painted overall in brown or tan and edged in gilding?
6. Is the hair pale and in thickish strands?
7. Does the figure have large numbers incised on the base?
8. Is the mark larger than in earlier periods?

Count Camillo Marcolini (1774–1813)

In 1774 Marcolini was appointed director of Meissen, heralding a move from the Rococo. Neo-classicism was introduced along with silhouettes, biscuit figures, Classical reliefs, and miniature paintings on solid grounds in the styles of Angelica Kauffmann. He also created a new fashion for underglaze blue, but he failed to make a profit and was dismissed in 1813.

• Meissen decorations at this time were among the best ever painted in Europe.

• The complex, but narrow gilt borders, as seen on these plates are very typical of this era. They do not follow the lines of the moulding and seem to have been added, almost as an afterthought. The gilding around the moulded cartouche is the same. The lively, naturalistic groupings of flowers and vegetables is typically Meissen, however. The bright glaze shows the glassier look seen at this time.

*A Marcolini porcelain tureen
and stand. c.1775 E*

At this stage, the dominant colour is pale pink rather than puce, and the painting is more romantic and less academic. Broad bands of gilding and grooved handles of square sections, often with shaped terminals, are typical of wares produced during the Marcolini period.

*Meissen porcelain soup plates. c.1780
9in (23cm) wide G*

*This mark
c.1750*

*This mark Marcolini
Meissen c.1774–1813*

*A mid 18thC Meissen
"Atlas". 6in (15.5cm)
high C*

Meissen figures

*A Meissen group
of a shepherd
and shepherdess,
modelled by
J. J. Kändler. c.1740
6in (15.5cm) high D*

1. Are the figures separately modelled?
2. Is the facial expression a bit severe but subtly painted?
3. Is the modelling very detailed?
4. Is the hair finely detailed in black?
5. Does the base have applied flowers or Rococo scrolls?
6. If the mark is not on the base is it on the back or the side?

Johann Joachim Kändler (1706–75)

Meissen first began figure production under Johann Jakob Kirchner, who was joined by Kändler in 1731. Kändler's talents eclipsed his master and Kirchner left in 1733. Kändler was to become the greatest of all the porcelain modellers. Kändler studied from life, producing animated figures that became popular decorations for the dinner table. These decorations became the factory's most sought-after products.

Kändler figures

The earliest figures represented ladies and gentlemen of the court and characters from the Italian Commedia dell'Arte, including the popular series of Harlequins modelled between 1738 and 1744. Other sets of figures include:
- peasants in national costume
- shepherds and shepherdesses
- mythological subjects
- The Cries of Paris
- The Cries of London
- Chinese and Middle Eastern figures
- animals and birds, particularly parrots.

A Meissen figure, "Giangurgolo", c.1745 6in (15.5cm) high C

A Meissen Turkish woman. 1744 6in (15.5cm) high D

Marks

The earliest Kändler figures were often glazed and marked on the underside. However, by 1740 the bases were usually unglazed and they painted a very small mark on the back or on the side of a figure. The early Kändler figures are set on pad bases or on mounds with applied flowers, and their strong colours are painted on in large washes, but the figures made after the late 1740s, such as this "Monkey Band" figure (see below), are dominated by pastel colours and stand on heavier bases decorated with Rococo scrolls. The faces on Kändler's figures are traditionally a bit severe but the colouring remains very subtle.

A Meissen "Monkey Band" double bass player, modelled by J.J. Kändler and Peter Reinicke. c.1765 4.75in (12cm) high E

19thC Meissen

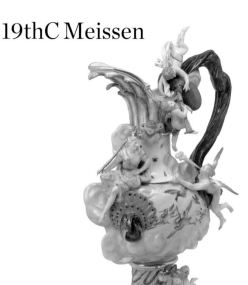

*A Meissen porcelain "Air"
element jug, 1818–60
26in (66cm) high D*

1. Is the piece heavily encrusted with flowers?
2. Does it have a key fret moulded base?
3. Do figures have lace work?
4. Do figures look more coy, almost simpering, than earlier ones?
5. Do the colours look rich, almost gaudy?
6. Is the overall look heavy and a little showy?
7. Are there large, cursive inscribed numbers?
8. Are there small, serif impressed numbers?

A late 19thC Meissen figure. 17in (43cm) high C

A pair of 19thC Meissen parrots. 13in (33cm) high E

Later porcelain

For a time after Marcolini's departure in 1813 the factory continued with Neo-classicism, but in the 1830s it returned to a new era of Rococo styles, which Meissen stuck to until the 1920s when they produced a number of stylish and innovative figures.

Marks

The crossed swords of the Marcolini period are larger and longer than on earlier products. They have a star between the hilts, and sometimes the Roman numerals I or II have been added below.

• After Marcolini the star was no longer used (see p.37).

• The stiff, elongated posture and crisply detailed drapery are characteristic of this period.

• The broad washes of pastel colours were used particularly on Classical figures. Contemporary figures were decorated with stripes or tiny florets. Like many wares from the late 19thC, the figure of a tailor (see above left), is 18thC in style.

• Like other factories, Meissen covered the whole surface, rather than confining it to a small reserve.

• Many of Meissen's 19thC revivals of 18thC figures, such as these parrots (see above right), have clumsy Rococo bases and rather washed out tones, which contrast dramatically with the sharper delineation and bolder colours of the 18thC.

• Extensive use of lace work, made from real lace dipped in clay, often gives late figures a fussy

A 19thC Meissen vase and cover. 26in (66cm) high D

Hausmaler

A Meissen "Goldchinesen" teapot and cover, decorated in the Augsburg workshop of Abraham Seuter. c.1725 4.5in (11.5cm) high B

1. Is the porcelain Meissen?
2. Is the piece decorated in monochrome?
3. Is the decoration a bit too large-scale for the vessel?
4. Is the piece completely decorated in chinoiserie gilding? (Seuter)
5. Is the overglaze decoration incompatible with the underglaze decoration? (Ferner)
6. Are there birds or flowers on the rim? (Meyer)

Hausmaler

Independent *Hausmaler* (home painters) bought wares in the white from the Meissen factory and decorated them in their own workshops, often decades after they were made. The most prolific of the recognizable *Hausmalerei* were Abraham and Bartholomaus Seuter from Augsburg known for their gilt chinoiserie silhouettes with elaborate scrolled and trellised consoles, highlighted with chiselled details, such as this teapot (see opposite).

• The Seuters almost always used borders composed of small cogged, or toothed, scrolls. Much of their work was carried out on unmarked porcelain dating from the 1720s.

Ignaz Preissler mainly worked in monochrome. His favourite subjects

A Meissen Hausmaler *teapot and cover, painted by Meyer von Pressnitz. c.1745 5.25in (13cm) wide G*

were town and landscapes, hunting and battle scenes, mythological scenes and chinoiseries surrounded by Baroque *Laub und Bandelwerk*-interlaced ornament consisting of foliage and strapwork. Franz Ferdinand Meyer, who worked in Bohemia from the late 1740s to the 1770s, was a prolific decorator mainly of plates, often landscapes in a subdued palette (see below).

A Meissen Böttger chocolate cup, painted by a Hausmaler *from Bayreuth. c.1719 2.5in (6.5cm) high F*

A Meissen Hausmaler *plate, painted by Franz Ferdinand Meyer. c.1745 8.75in (22.5cm) diam E*

43

Vienna Du Paquier

A Du Paquier cup and saucer. 1725–30. Cup 2.5in (6.5cm) high E

1. Is the porcelain hard-paste?
2. Is the glaze thin and slightly green?
3. Are the reserves in the decoration shaped like Chinese lanterns?
4. Do the scenes in the decoration have a deep perspective?
5. Does the decoration contain latticework with tiny star-like flowers at the intersections?
6. Does it also include moulded fleurs-de-lys?
7. Is it in monochrome?

Du Paquier, (1718–44)

Claudius Innocentius du Paquier founded Europe's second porcelain factory in Vienna in 1717. He bribed Christoph Conrad Hunger from Meissen for the secret of arcanum. The greyish-white Vienna hard-paste is like the Meissen, but sometimes slightly bluer and smokier. The glaze, which has a slightly green tone, is generally much thinner and less glassy than Meissen. Once out, the secret of porcelain making did not stay long in Vienna and soon spread to Höchst, Frankenthal, Ludwigsburg, and Ellwangen.

Style

Du Paquier's porcelain reflected the grandeur and exuberance of a Baroque city and the shapes are distinctive. Du Paquier's *Laub und Bandelwerk* (leaf and strapwork), which was initially used to decorate borders, gradually evolved

A Du Paquier cup and saucer. c.1735 2.5in (6.5cm) high E

into complex geometric patterns. Latticework filled the reserves, and star-like flowers were added.

Schwarzlot

Many of du Paquier's pieces (like this cup and saucer, see above) were decorated in monochrome, known as *Schwarzlot*. Du Paquier made only a few figures, often small and stiff and based on Chinese styles or Commedia dell'Arte characters.

A Vienna Du Paquier white-glazed elephant decanter. c.1730 19.25in (49cm) long AA

A Du Paquier beaker. c.1720 2.5in (6.5cm) high D

Vienna 1744–84

*A Vienna Imperial
Manufactory white figure.
c.1760 8in (20.5cm) high F*

1. Is the porcelain hard-paste and greyish?
2. Is the glaze white and glassy?
3. Do the shapes of the wares follow Meissen or, if not, are they decorated in Imari colours?
4. If a hollow figure, is it without a base?
5. If the figure has a mound base, does it look as though it has been hacked with a knife?
6. Is the base decorated with a triangular gilt pattern?
7. Does the figure have a mark accompanied by incised numbers and letters?

Vienna (1744–84)

In 1744, du Paquier's factory was taken over by the state and continued to produce older shapes and patterns but introduced new Rococo tablewares in the Meissen style. During this time Vienna had some of the best enamellers, including Johann Gottfried Klinger, who came from Meissen in 1746 and stayed until 1781. By far the most important products during the "State" period were figures, especially those by Niedermayer, who was master modeller from 1747–84.

A late 18thC Vienna figure. 6.5in (16.5cm) high H

Paste and glaze

From 1749 onwards the Vienna factory used a much finer Hungarian clay, although the paste is still slightly grey. The State period glaze is white but glassy.

A late 18thC Vienna figure. 7.5in (19cm) high G

A Vienna plate. c.1765 9in (23cm) diam F

Palette

The most dominant colours are green and pale mauve or lilac. Three other colours are also prominent: • puce
• lemon yellow
• egg-yolk yellow.

This figure of a lady (see below) is typical of State period figures with its slightly stiff posture, full-cheeked face, blushed cheeks, rouged lips, and triangular gilding pattern. In the 1760s, Rococo bases were replaced by pie-like pads that look as though they have been hacked with a knife. Some figures are washed in greens and browns or are seen without bases. During the mid-18thC the Vienna factory produced Imari wares, copying designs from Japan, even adding a blue tinge to the glaze, but the painting is more mechanical. During the State period, the Vienna factory adopted the Austrian shield as its mark.

Vienna 1784–1864

*A Vienna Imperial
Manufactory plate,
depicting "Diana and
Endymion". 1823
9in (23cm) diam D*

1. Is the porcelain hard-paste?
2. Do wares have three impressed date numerals?
3. Is the shape Neo-classical?
4. Does the decoration cover all the exterior porcelain?
5. Is the gilding very high quality with matt and burnished surface details?
6. Can you feel the gilding?
7. Does the piece have more than one coloured ground?
8. Is it decorated with Classical subjects in the manner of Angelica Kauffmann or painted with realistic and large-scale flowers?

Vienna (1784–1864)

In 1784 with the factory in serious financial difficulties, Konrad Sorgel von Sorgenthal was appointed director. He abandoned the Rococo old-fashioned style and embraced Neo-classicism with solid coloured grounds and gilt scrollwork in the style of Sèvres.

Paste and glaze

Vienna's glaze was subtly different: warmer and not as glassy as Berlin, Paris, and Meissen.

Wares

During this period, the factory's success largely depended on its richly gilded services, tea and coffee wares, and its decorative wares, which had clean lines where surface modelling was restricted.

• The gilding of this period is often tooled or engraved – a feature that was much copied by other factories in the late 19thC.

A small Vienna epergne with lid. 1810 6in (15.5cm) high G

Fewer figures were made in this period and were usually in biscuit. Common subjects were busts or copies of Classical statues. The botanical painting on Vienna porcelain is among the very best of the period. Other wares produced at Vienna include "named view" plates with topographical scenes painted in minute detail.

A Vienna Imperial Manufactory porcelain Anton Schaller cup and saucer, Sorgenthal period. c.1800 Saucer 5.2in (13cm) diam E

A Vienna cup and saucer. 1795 Saucer 5in (12.5cm) diam F

Late 19thC Vienna

A late 19thC Vienna porcelain vase, painted with Napoleonic scenes. 29in (73.5cm) high C

1. Is the gilding printed?
2. If it has a Classical scene is it a lithograph?
3. Are there any other factory marks?
4. Is there evidence of a factory mark being painted (or gilded) over?
5. Is the porcelain thin and almost egg-shell like?
6. Is the style of figure painting a little too sentimental?
7. Are the shapes fussy and overly showy?
8. Has the "Vienna" mark been rubber-stamped (see opposite) or does it look smudged?

A late 19thC Vienna porcelain plaque.
8.5in (21.5cm) high F

A late 19thC Vienna plaque.
24.25in (61.5cm) diam D

Following the closure of the Vienna factory in 1864 its popular style was continued, and some would say debased, by other factories, many of which were in Germany or Bohemia. These later pieces were popular into the early 20thC and range from high-quality pieces, often painted on old stock by ex-employees, to cheap transfer-printed and lithographed examples on thin, egg-shell bodies. The later the piece the more it will have strayed away from the true Vienna style. The majority of these are in the Neo-classical style, but towards 1900, more contemporary styles were seen, often sentimental in subject. The often lavish style of these later pieces has made them very popular with collectors.

Many of these later pieces bear the Vienna Shield mark, which is often inverted, hence its popular name of the "Bee-hive" mark. Later marks are often printed or rubber-stamped.

This mark
late 19thC to early
20thC

A late 19thC Vienna vase,
signed "Schlesinger",
entitled "Summerlust".
15.5in (39.5cm) high E

Frankenthal

*A Frankenthal coffee pot, for
the court of Kurpfalz. c.1759
10in (25.5cm) high A*

1. Is the porcelain hard-paste?
2. Is it fine and white?
3. Is the glaze creamy or slightly grey and a bit grainy?
4. Is the piece the shape of silverware?
5. Do the cups have flare mouthrims?
6. Do the plates have basketweave borders?
7. If a pot, is the cover flush with the body of the vessel?
8. Are the figures in the decoration larger than on other wares?
9. Do the figures have more movement than on other wares?
10. Is there a lot of gilding?

A Frankenthal plate, mark of Joseph-Adam Hannong. c.1759 9in (23cm) diam G

A butter dish. c.1760 5.5in (14cm) diam G

Frankenthal (1755–99)

In 1751, Paul-Antoine Hannong began producing hard-paste porcelain at his Strasbourg faïence works to such a standard that in 1753 King Louis XV ordered him to stop. Undaunted, Hannong moved to Frankenthal, where the Elector Karl Theodor granted him a monopoly.

Paste and glaze

Early Frankenthal has a fine, white hard-paste, which after 1774 declined. The well-fused, creamy-grey glaze is opaque and a bit "musliny". The glaze is also unusual in that it absorbs the enamel colours, giving the porcelain the overall effect of soft-paste, rather than resistant hard-paste.

Wares

Early wares are French in style and often silver-shaped. Cups tend to have subtly flared rims. Handles are usually plain loops with lower terminals shaped like acanthus leaves, or else exaggerated "C" scrolls with reversed curved brackets.

Decoration

Typical themes are:
• landscapes with Classical ruins with foliage or giltwork
• figures after Watteau or Boucher
• delicate flower painting with outspread tendrils in the style of Strasbourg (see plate above left)
The figures on this coffee pot (see left) are typical. They are painted much larger in scale and the gilding is extensive.

Palette

The 1760s palette is typified by green and purple. Other important colours are:
• puce
• yellowish green
• greyish yellow
• ultramarine
• greyish blue
• chestnut brown

A Frankenthal teapot and cover. c.1770 4.5in (11.5cm) high E

This mark 1759–76

Frankenthal figures

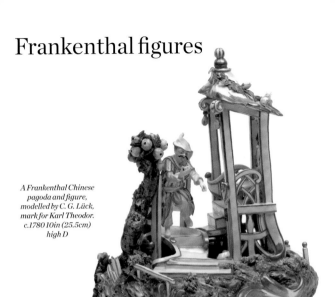

A Frankenthal Chinese pagoda and figure, modelled by C. G. Lück, mark for Karl Theodor. c.1780 10in (25.5cm) high D

1. Is the porcelain hard-paste?
2. Is the glaze creamy, thin, and opaque?
3. Is the figure stiffly modelled?
4. Is the modelling quite detailed?
5. Are the features small and doll-like?
6. Are the hands oversized?
7. Does the figure have an undulating base with gilt or puce scrolls on it?
8. Does the base have arched edges?
9. Are there tufts of green moss on the base?

Frankenthal figures

Frankenthal figures are stiffly modelled, have small, features, big eyes, rouged cheeks, and oversized hands. They have quite detailed modelling, which the thin, opaque glaze does not obscure.

J. A. Hannong (1734–c.1800)

In 1759, Paul-Antoine Hannong sold the factory to his son Joseph-Adam Hannong but in 1762, the Elector Karl Theodor bought the factory, closing it in 1794.

Modellers

The first chief modeller was Johann Wilhelm Lanz who introduced an undulating Rococo base with puce or gilt scrolls. Johann Frederick Lück arrived from Höchst at the end of the 1750s followed by his cousin Karl Gottlieb. During State ownership, the court

A Frankenthal figure of a woman, modelled by J. F. Lück. c.1760 5.5in (14cm) high E

A Frankenthal figure. c.1767 5in (12.5cm) high F

sculptor, Konrad Linck, became chief modeller, introducing Neo-classicism. Linck modified the traditional factory base, making it a more simple brown mound with tufts of green moss.

Marks

The main mark used was the monogram shown below. Between 1770 and 1788 the last two numerals of the date were added. From 1755 to 1756 the mark was "PH" for Paul Hannong, sometimes followed by a lion rampant and the quartered chequered shield of the Palatinate in blue. From 1759 to 1762 the letters JAH were used for Joseph-Adam Hannong.

This mark for Carl Theodor 1780–93

An 18thC Frankenthal vase. 14in (35.5cm) high F

Höchst

A Höchst teapot, by Andreas Philipp Oettner. c.1760 4.5in (11.5cm) high E

1. Is the porcelain hard-paste?
2. Does it have a glassy and creamy-white glaze similar to faïence?
3. Is the material generally free from flaws?
4. Is there a predominance of green and puce in the colour scheme?
5. If it is a Rococo teapot, is it bullet-shaped with a knop in the form of a closed bud?
6. Does the pot have a wishbone handle with two projecting thumbpieces?
7. Do cups and bowls have slightly outcurved rims?
8. Is the piece marked with a wheel (see opposite)?

A Höchst tea caddy. c.1767 4.5in (11.5cm) high F

Höchst (1746–96)

Adam Friedrich von Löwenfink established Höchst in 1746, but the factory was never financially secure. It was saved from bankruptcy in 1778, but despite the quality of its wares decline continued until its closure in 1796.

Höchst hard-paste porcelain is pure white, generally free from flaws, and covered in a glassy, dead-white or creamy glaze, which sometimes looks almost like a highly refined faïence. Teapots in the early Rococo style are a compact "bullet" shape (see opposite). Their lids are flush with the body and have closed-bud knops. Handles are "wishbone" in shape and have two projecting thumbpieces and scroll terminals.

Cups have slightly outcurved rims. The handles on the cups are plain loops, again with scrolled terminals. Landscapes and seascapes were popular. On some, such as this tea caddy c.1767 (see above left), the scene is framed by delicate gilt cartouches. Other decorative themes include:

• flowers
• chinoiseries
• scenes after Teniers
• figure subjects
• battle scenes
• hunting scenes
• *fêtes galantes*.

The standard of painting on Höchst wares is very high. Among the best artists were the founder's brother, Christian Wilhelm von Löwenfink, the painter Johannes Zeschinger, Joseph Philipp Danhofer, and Joseph Angele. Wares usually have neat incised numbers or letters inside the base identifying the workmen. The Höchst mark is a wheel taken from the Mainz coat of arms, which until c.1765 was painted in overglaze colours. After this date the mark is seen in underglaze blue.

A Höchst plate. c.1782 10in (25.5cm) diam E

This mark c.1765–74

Höchst figures

A Höchst figure group, modelled by Johann Peter Melchior. c.1770 6.5in (16.5cm) high E

1. Is the porcelain hard-paste?
2. Is the material generally free from flaws?
3. Is the figure painted in pastel shades?
4. Does it have childlike features?
5. If a group, are the figures gathered around fantastic rock- or trelliswork?
6. Is the figure set on a high Rococo-scroll base or a grassy knoll?
7. Are there incised marks on the base?

Höchst figures

The early Höchst figures tend to be very static with strong colours. Like this pair of hunters (see below), they have none of the movement, complexity, romanticism, and subtle colouring that were to make the later models so distinctive.

18thC Höchst figures. 7.25in (18.5cm) high E

Johann Peter Melchior (1742–1825)

The later figures created by Johann Peter Melchior sealed Höchst's reputation. Influenced by Rousseau and Boucher, he concentrated on pastoral models and sentimental groups of children in pastel shades. His eye detail and his ability to recreate a mood set him among the greatest 18thC modellers. Melchior arrived at Höchst in 1765, becoming master modeller two years later. The Elector decided to appoint him court sculptor to prevent other princes from enticing him away. He became a favourite at court, where he formed a friendship with the poet Goethe. When the Elector died, the factory

managers reduced his wages, and in 1779 he moved on to the Frankenthal factory.

Marks

Höchst figures bear the wheel mark that is often accompanied by incised letters or numbers, which were probably used to identify the workman who "repaired" or assembled the figures from their parts.

Copies

The wheel mark is not conclusive proof that a figure is Höchst. Look out for faïence copies from Damm, in the late 19thC, and porcelain versions from Poppelsdorf and Passau at the beginning of the 20thC.

A pair of 18thC Höchst figures of a hunter and his companion. 6.75in (17cm) high E

Ludwigsburg

*A Ludwigsburg teapot
with lid, with Schwarzlot
decoration. 1758–93.
7.5in (16cm) high G*

1. Is the piece hard-paste?
2. Is the glaze smoky?
3. If the piece is a teapot, is it bullet-shaped with a fruit knop and a flush or recessed cover?
4. Is the mouth of the spout shaped like a bird's head?
5. If the piece is a cup, does it have a "C"-shaped scroll?
6. If the piece is a saucer, is it quite flared?
7. If the decoration is a landscape, are there two or three tufts of foliage hanging from its base?
8. Is the piece moulded with an overall scale diaper, a band of basketweave, or a frieze of rectangular panels?
9. Is the mark right (see opposite)?

A Ludwigsburg tea canister. c.1770
4in (10cm) high G

Ludwigsburg (1758/9–1824)

Ludwigsburg was established by Carl Eugen, Duke of Württemberg, under the direction of J. J. Ringler. The paste is greyish-white and close-grained, and the glaze can often be smoky.

Teawares

Teapots are usually bullet-shaped, like Höchst's, but with fruit-shaped knops. The spouts can have mouths shaped like birds or dragons. Ludwigsburg cups have "C"-shaped scroll handles with protruding thumb-pieces like tiny shells or feathers. Most of them also have dark brown or enamel rims. Ludwigsburg saucers are usually quite flared.

Figure painting

A Ludwigsburg porcelain coffee pot and cover. c.1780
5.75in (14.5cm) H

can be wooden and puppet-like in puce and deep russet as on this tea canister. Ludwigsburg landscapes have two or three tufts of foliage around the base – only seen elsewhere at Fürstenberg and Worcester painted by Fidèle Duvivier.

Marks

The standard mark from 1758 to 1793 is a ducal crown above the interlaced "C"s – the cipher of Carl Eugen. It is neater than the similar mark of Niderviller, which is usually much more loosely executed. Other, rarer marks include a crown and initials "FR" or "WR" for kings Frederick and William respectively; and the stags' antlers from the arms of Württemberg, sometimes arranged in a group of three. Most marks are drawn in underglaze blue but there are also a few that have been gilded or drawn in iron red or black. The Ludwigsburg marks are rarely seen impressed.

A Ludwigsburg porcelain pipe bowl, moulded as a Turk's face. c.1760
2.75in (7cm) high F

This mark c.1758–93

Ludwigsburg figures

*A Ludwigsburg
figure group, for
Carl Eugen Herzog
von Württemberg.
c.1765 6in (15.5cm)
high F*

1. Is the piece hard-paste?
2. Is the glaze a smoky grey colour?
3. Is the piece stiff but crisply modelled?
4. Is it decorated in subdued pastel shades?
5. Is the face characterless?
6. If a miniature, is it an animated and brightly painted group?
7. Is the mark right (see p.61)?

Ludwigsburg figures

Former director of painting at Frankenthal, Gottlieb Friedrich Riedel, was responsible for the creation of elegant Rococo figures that were among the finest of Ludwigsburg's products. Occasionally naïve, they are crisply modelled and precisely decorated in pastel colours, which blend with the smoky tone of the glaze. Some of the best were modelled by the architect, painter, and court sculptor Johann Christian Wilhelm Beyer, who was overseer of the modelling workshop from about 1764 to 1767. In the 1790s several models were made by the great Neo-classical sculptor Johann Heinrich von Dannecker, but by then the factory was in decline. After a brief revival at the beginning of the following century, it closed in 1824.

Palette

The principal colours in Ludwigsburg's restrained Rococo palette are:

- greyish puce
- greyish cobalt
- greyish green
- yellow
- iron red
- mid-brown
- black
- gilding.

Bases

There is a surprising variety of bases on Ludwigsburg figures; these range from simple grass or rockwork mounds and slabs, highlighted in washed-out green or russet, to expensive and complicated Rococo compositions with deeply moulded "C" scrolls picked out in gilding. Miniature groups are among the most famous of all the Ludwigsburg figures. Although less than 3in/7.5cm in height, they are much more animated than the larger figures. The first series, designed by Riedel, represented scenes from the Venetian fair, which was held annually by the Duke and his court following the Duke's visit to Italy in 1767. This was followed by groups by Beyer representing daily life.

A Ludwigsburg figure group. c.1770 6.5in (16.5cm) high F

A Ludwigsburg "Print Seller" figure, modelled by J. J. Louis. c.1766 6in (15.5cm) high E

Nymphenburg

A Nymphenburg plate.
c.1765 9in (23cm)
diam G

1. Is the porcelain hard-paste?
2. Is it free of imperfections?
3. Is the glaze a greyish colour, but a greenish cream in places where it has pooled?
4. Is the piece marked with an impressed shield?
5. Is the decoration particularly skilfully and sensitively painted?
6. Does it represent birds on branches or loose bouquets of flowers?
7. If the piece is a tea cup, does it have complex, ear-shaped handles?
8. If the piece is a teapot, is it shaped like a truncated pear, with a swan's head spout and a tube projecting from its beak?

Nymphenburg (1747–present)

Although Max Joseph II of Bavaria opened the factory in 1747, porcelain was not produced in earnest until 1753. In 1761, the factory was moved to the palace at Nymphenburg, where it has remained ever since.

Paste and glaze

The best Nymphenburg porcelain belongs to the early period, until c.1770. The hard-paste is white, close-grained, and flawless, the glaze warm and wet-looking.

Designs

Nymphenburg is well known for tea and coffee services and other wares. Teapots made between 1755 and 1765 are easily recognized. The spout is long and of swan's neck form It often has what looks like a tube projecting from the beak.

Decoration

The decoration on Nymphenburg wares

A Nymphenburg cup and saucer. 1858 Cup 3.5in (9cm) high E

This mark 1820–47

is usually very skilfully and sensitively painted. The finest and most popular type depicts birds in the branches of trees or loose bouquets of flowers, such as those on the plates shown opposite. In the early 19thC the factory followed Sèvres and imitated the Neo-classical French Empire style.

Palette

The Nymphenburg palette consists of:
• ochre
• puce
• mushroom pink
• sky blue
• greyish, almost olive green
• yellow
• brownish red
• brown
• gilding.

Marks

Nymphenburg porcelain is marked with an impressed shield derived from the *Rautensschild* of Bavaria.

A Nymphenburg lidded terrine. c.1770 10in (22.5cm) high E

Nymphenburg figures

A Nymphenburg figure "A Chinese Boy", modelled by Franz Anton Bustelli. c.1757 5in (12.5cm) high E

1. Is the porcelain hard-paste?
2. Is it free from imperfections?
4. Does the figure grow from its base?
5. Is the base flat with slight Rococo curves at the edges?
5. Is the lower part of the figure a bit elongated?
6. Is it exceptionally light in weight?
7. Are the folds on the clothes sharply defined?
8. Is the figure marked with an impressed shield?

Franz Anton Bustelli (1722–63)

The finest of all the Nymphenburg products are the figures modelled by Franz Anton Bustelli, who as a modeller for porcelain was second only to J. J. Kändler at Meissen. The 150 figures that he modelled during his eight and a half years at Nymphenburg are works of genius.

Style

Bustelli was the master of the Rococo. His figures are detached and ethereal; they have none of the slightly cruel realism that characterizes the German work. The lower parts of the models are a little elongated, but they have expressive faces and contrast between flowing lines and busy surfaces.

Subjects

Apart from allegorical figures and characters from the Commedia dell'Arte, Bustelli's most important subjects were: Chinese characters and scenes; Turks and Moors; ladies and gentlemen;

merchants and street vendors; shepherds and shepherdesses; religious subjects; and dogs and cats.

Bases

Unlike the figures of other modellers, which look as though they have been attached to their bases, Bustelli's figures seem to grow out of them. The earliest figures stand on flat bases with slight, asymmetrical Rococo curves at the edges.

Dominikus Jakob Auliczek

After Bustelli's death his successor, Dominikus Jakob Auliczek, added more animal figures, including several brutal hunting groups that depict hounds attacking their prey.

A Nymphenburg figure of "Lucinda", from the Commedia Dell'Arte, model no. 69, by F. A. Bustelli. c.1760 7.5in (18cm) high F

A Nymphenburg putto, modelled by Franz Anton Bustelli. 1758 4.25in (11cm) high G

A Nymphenburg figure of a hunter on horseback. c.1765 7.5in (19cm) high H

Fürstenberg

A Fürstenberg gilt-metal-mounted snuff box and cover.
c.1770 E

1. Is the porcelain hard-paste?
2. Is the glaze off-white and glittery?
3. Is the palette dominated by dark browns and greens?
4. Is the piece decorated in monochrome purple or green?
5. Is the piece decorated with moulded ribbonwork?
6. Does it have elaborate moulding?
7. Are the handles on cups and pots formed by an exaggerated "C" scroll on a small inverted crescent, or are they ear-shaped?
8. Is the rim of the piece decorated with flimsy scrollwork and a spider's web motif?
9. If the piece is a pot, does it have galleried rims on the cover, below the neck and around the base?

Fürstenberg (1753–c.1800)

The Duke of Brunswick established a factory at Fürstenberg in 1747, producing porcelain from 1753, when the management was entrusted to Johann Benekgraff, until then the manager of the factory at Höchst.

Paste and glaze

The Fürstenberg hard-paste is close-grained and white, and looks very similar to the body of Meissen or Berlin. The glaze is off-white and glittery. Early pieces may have elaborate moulded scrollwork to disguise flaws in the paste.

Decoration

Many decorations were painted in a single colour, known as *en camaïeu* and are either enclosed in contrasting scrolls or unframed. Landscapes are often on a slightly larger scale in relation to the size of the vessel. Most are based on Flemish engravings.

Palette

The palette is dominated by browns and greens.

The main colours are:
• dark, reddish brown
• tan
• iron red
• chrome yellow
• dirty turquoise
• puce
• lilac
• dark green
• yellowish green
• grey green
• greyish blue
• gilding (used copiously).

Much of Fürstenberg's decoration was behind the times; it can be heavy, with incongruous elements, such as a mix of Neo-classical and Rococo themes. Meticulous vignettes of poultry and other birds perched on branches or fences, painted by C. G. Albert, are typically Fürstenberg. Fürstenberg produced a large number of Neo-classical wares painted with monochrome or slightly drab panels.

A Fürstenberg vase and cover. c.1785 16.5in (42cm) high F

A late 18thC Fürstenberg cup and saucer. Cup 2.5in (6.5cm) high F

A Fürstenberg bullet-shaped teapot and cover. c.1770 G

Fürstenberg figures

A Fürstenberg group, "Hercules, Omphale and Amor", modelled by Anton Carl Luplau. c.1775 7.5in (19cm) high C

1. Is the porcelain hard-paste?
2. Does it contain small black flecks?
3. Are figures set on simple pad or mound bases?
4. Are the groups set on elaborate scroll bases?
5. Are the figures rather stiff with pursed lips and severe expressions?
6. Are the subjects stockily built?
7. If the figure is a miner, has it been left in the white?

Fürstenberg figures

Fürstenberg made a number of Classical figures based on bronze or ivories which may account for the fine crisp modelling. Others were based on models from other factories such as Berlin, Höchst, and particularly Meissen. Fürstenberg figures are more compact than other factories and like the figures opposite, they have highly coloured, fleshy skin.

Subjects

Fürstenberg was known for depicting miners, Classical gods, and contemporary costumes; the finest were modelled by Simon Feilner. His early figures have characteristically Fürstenberg pursed lips and disapproving expressions. They were set on plain, pad bases decorated with flowers. The paste is flawed and has small black flecks. Figures tend to have a large cross-shaped support beneath the bases. Desoches and Hendler were also modellers at Fürstenberg in the 1770s.

A pair of Fürstenberg ostriches, modelled by Simon Feilner. 1754 6.75in (17cm) high D

This mark c.1753–80

Their figures have prettier faces with even features. Hendler's figures have stiffer bodies and are not anatomically correct.

Copies

The Fürstenberg factory carried on into the 19thC, when the original 18thC moulds were used to produce clumsily decorated copies of the original figures.

Marks

The Fürstenberg mark is one of the simplest: a script capital "F" in underglaze blue. However, although some versions are very straightforward, others are very hastily written and barely recognizable. Neo-classical figures, particularly biscuit busts, were sometimes impressed with a horse from the arms of Brunswick.

A Fürstenberg group, "Asia and Africa", modelled by Anton Carl Luplau. c.1773 6.25in (16cm) high D

Fulda

A Fulda cup and saucer.
c.1775 F

1. Is the paste almost flawless?
2. Is the glaze warm and creamy?
3. If the piece is a ware, is it decorated with a landscape vignette with trailing foliage and roots?
4. Is the decoration framed or partially framed by puce and russet-brown feathered scrolls?
5. Is the foreground predominantly deep brown?
6. Are the handles on vessels formed in a treble scroll?
7. Are painted landscapes reminiscent of Meissen?
8. Is the modelling of figures very detailed but a little stiff?
9. Does the figure have a doll-like face with rosy cheeks, a tiny nose, and pinpoint eyes?

Fulda (1764–90)

In 1764 Johann Philipp Schick began to make porcelain at his faïence factory in Fulda, hiring Nikolaus Paul who had worked at the Weesp factory in Holland to oversee production. Paul stayed for only a year and despite its high-quality wares, the factory only lasted until 1790.

Wares

All the Fulda products are made with great care and skill and were in the Meissen tradition. Fulda wares do have distinguishing features. On early wares (see jug below) the landscapes are vignettes with autumnal brown foliage and roots hanging down from the scene like seaweed. On later wares, landscape and figure subjects (which may be painted *en camaïeu*) are partially or completely enclosed within a frame of elaborately feathered Rococo scrolls. The handles on many vessels are formed in a treble scroll. After about 1775, the factory turned to the Neo-classical style.

Palette

The Fulda palette consists mostly of:
- greyish blue
- green
- egg-yolk yellow
- orange
- rust brown
- iron red
- puce
- black
- gilding.

A Fulda white-glazed figure of a boy, personifying winter. c.1775 7.5in (19cm) high F

Figures

Among the finest Fulda figures are the characters from the Commedia dell'Arte, modelled by Wenzel Neu, and the series of the Fulda court orchestra and the Cries of Paris, modelled by G. L. Bartoleme.

Marks

Between 1764 and 1780, the mark was a cross in underglaze blue. From 1781 to 1788, the mark was a crown over an upper case, double script "F". During the last year of the factory's life, the "F"s were interlaced.

A pear-shaped Fulda jug, with "C"-scroll handle. c.1785 6in (15.5cm) high F

Minor Thuringian factories

A Limbach figure group, "Venus and Armor". c.1770 8.75in (22cm) high E

1. Is the porcelain hard-paste?
2. Is it on the whole a bit grey?
3. Is the piece trying to pass itself off as Meissen or, alternatively, is it an obvious copy of some other factory, such as Wedgwood?
4. If a figure, does it have naïve, doll-like features?
5. Is the modelling of the figure crude?

The Thuringian factories

The nine small factories in the Saxon province of Thuringia were established in the third quarter of the 18thC. This was at a time when the most famous German factories had reached their prime or even passed it. Like all the great German factories however, the most important in Thuringia, which was Closter-Veilsdorf, was founded by a prince. The other factories were founded by merchants and amateur chemists, whose down-to-earth business instincts kept them going long after many of the more creative establishments had been forced to close. Although the only pieces with any artistic merit were made during the last quarter of the 18thC, some of the factories survived into the 19thC and 20thC, producing unaffected figures of peasants, numerous copies of figures from other German factories, and

A Thuringian model, "Harlequin", playing the bagpipes. c.1770 5in (12.5cm) high G

A Volkstedt tea caddy. c.1780 4.25in (11cm) high H

simple, highly commercial but usually second-rate tableware.

A 19thC Volkstedt porcelain figural group. 6.75in (17cm) high G

A Limbach figure of "Autumn", from a set of the Four Seasons. c.1775 6.75in (17cm) high F

Gotha (1757–1937)

Gotha may have been established as early as 1757, but it did not begin to flourish until 1767. Of all Thuringian porcelain, the porcelain made by Gotha is the most carefully decorated. The paste is light and transparent, and the glaze is very soft and creamy. The best pieces are: wares decorated with polychrome flowers or pastoral scenes; presentation pieces, such as

fine silhouetted cups and mythological figures and busts made in an unglazed, marble-like, white porcelain.

Volkstedt (1760–1894)

The factory at Volkstedt was founded in 1760 by Georg Heinrich Macheleid, a clergyman with an interest in natural sciences. After discovering his own formula for making hard-paste porcelain he petitioned Johann Friederich, Fürst von Schwarzburg-Rudolstadt, who granted him a privilege to manufacture porcelain as part of his court. The Prince Schwarzburg-Rudolstadt eventually becoming the proprietor. The early hard-paste porcelain is heavy and grey and has an unclear glaze. Painters used flowers to hide the many bubbles and fire-cracks. Later porcelain is still flawed, but on many wares the flaws are camouflaged by the Rococo modelling. Many wares are crude copies of Meissen (see pp. 32–3). Volkstedt's hard-paste was well suited to modelling. As a result, some of its finest early products are bright and animated rural figures.

Wallendorf (1764–1833)

Wallendorf was established in 1764 by a group that included the cousins Johann Gottfried Greiner and Gotthelf Greiner. The porcelain they made is light and transparent, although the glaze is thick and yellowish. The figure modelling is clumsy. Specialities are pipe bowls and cups with no handles.

Gera (1779–1800)

Established in 1779, Gera was taken over after initial financial difficulties by Johann Georg Wilhelm and Johann Andreas, the sons of Johann Gottfried Greiner. Most products are Neo-classical. The porcelain is generally of poor quality although this is masked by decoration. One of the most characteristic decorations is a brown surface painted to represent wood.

Limbach (1772–1937)

Second in importance to Closter-Veilsdorf, Limbach was founded in 1772 by Gotthelf Greiner, from Wallendorf. The early porcelain is slightly yellow, but the later glaze has a lighter, more delicate quality. The most successful products are stiff, charmingly naïve figures. Most of them represent peasants and citizens and imaginary royalty in theatrical robes. The best of the early wares are superficial copies of Meissen, many marked deceptively with a pair of crossed "L's and a star. But in 1787, under pressure from Meissen, the mark was changed to a trefoil.

Ilmenau (1777–1990)

Founded in 1777, Ilmenau was leased by Gotthelf Greiner between 1782 and 1792, when he assigned it to the managership of Volkstedt. According to the poet Goethe, who decorated some wares himself, the paste was very poor quality. The factory made some blue and white imitations of Wedgwood.

Grossbreitenbach (c.1770–1800)

Established in the late 1770s, Grossbreitenbach was sold in 1782 to Gotthelf Greiner, who made it a branch of the Limbach factory.

Rauenstein (1783– c.1901)

Rauenstein was established in 1783. Most of the Rauenstein products, however, were copies.

An 18thC Wallendorf porcelain mustard pot and cover. 4in (10cm) high H

Closter-Veilsdorf

A pair of Closter-Veilsdorf Turkish figures, modelled by Pfanger senior. c.1770 7.75in (19.5cm) high D

1. Is the porcelain hard-paste?
2. Is the paste smooth, milk-white, and almost flawless (see opposite page)?
3. On pieces from tea and coffee sets, is the handle complex?
4. Is any moulding confined to the bottom half of the vessel?
5. Is the moulding basketweave, shells, or a flowery diaper?
6. On wares, is the painting detailed and realistic?
7. Is the landscape framed in drapery?
8. If the piece is a figure, is it small?

Closter-Veilsdorf (1760–present)

Established in 1760 by Prince Friedrich von Hildburghausen, Closter-Veilsdorf (also known as Kloster-Veilsdorf) was the most important Thuringian factory, which by 1795 was owned by the family of Gotthelf Greiner.

Early hard-paste

The early products of Closter-Veilsdorf are made of a very smooth, milk-white, almost unblemished porcelain with occasionally iron-spot flaws. After 1770, however, both paste and glaze became slightly grey.

Palette

The dominant colours at Closter-Veilsdorf are:

- pale puce
- iron red
- yellow
- greyish blue
- green
- grey.

Turquoise was apparently never used at Closter-Veilsdorf.

Wares

Before about 1780 the wares made at Closter-Veilsdorf

A Closter-Veilsdorf figure of Apollo. c.1765 6.25in (16 cm) high G

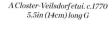

A Closter-Veilsdorf etui. c.1770 5.5in (14cm) long G

followed the general Rococo style used by most German and Austrian factories. The edges of wares are often heightened in puce. Handles are often eccentric confections involving many "C" scrolls. The factory's figures are usually small (not more than 7in/18cm) and simple – fingers are not separate. Faces are highly coloured, but lack character. The bases for the figures are simple mounds, sometimes lightly carved with scrolls. Wenzel Neu made some of its best figures between 1762 and 1767, when he returned to Fulda.

Decoration

The decorative themes on wares are conventional; some based on drawings by Prince Friedrich.

Marks

- The letters "C" and "V" in blue or in a monogram, sometimes with the shield of Saxony.
  - A three-petalled flower head, which is also found on Limbach and Grossbreitenbach wares.

Berlin

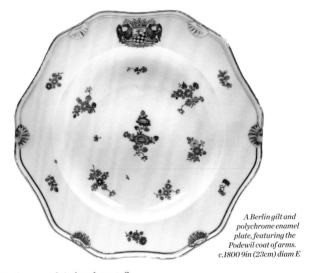

A Berlin gilt and polychrome enamel plate, featuring the Podewil coat of arms. c.1800 9in (23cm) diam E

1. Is the porcelain hard-paste?
2. Is it slightly greyish white with a creamy, opaque glaze?
3. Is the appearance glassy and bluish?
4. Does any enamel decoration display patches of flaking?
5. Is the piece moulded in any way?
6. Does it have rustic handles?
7. If a figure, is it set on a square, slab base?
8. Do the figure's feet project?
9. Are the marks right?

Berlin (1752–present)

The first factory, founded in 1752 by Wilhelm Kaspar Wegely, closed in 1757. However, the second, founded in 1761 by Johann Ernst Gotzkowsky, became one of the most influential of the 20thC.

Wegely paste and glaze

The early paste is of fine white porcelain, not unlike Meissen –in fact, both factories obtained most of their material from the same source. The glaze on this early ware is thin and colourless and tends to be opaque.

Wegely wares

Wegely produced decorative wares, such as vases, which were often liberally encrusted with flowers and human masks and with figures on the lids. Tea and coffee wares have moulded Oriental flowers, although some were plain-surfaced.

A KPM Berlin porcelain vase. c.1780 7.75in (19.5cm) high E

Wegely decoration

Decoration tended to follow the Meissen style, with landscapes, Watteau-esque figures and semi-botanical subjects. However, the glaze did not accept enamelling well, and in many cases small areas have flaked.

Wegely figures

Wegely produced a range of figures that were either copied from Meissen, such as cupids and Commedia dell'Arte characters, or created from printed sources, such as huntsmen and artisans.

A KPM Berlin figure, "Air", modelled by Friedrich Elias Meyer. c.1761–63 10in (25.5cm) high G

A Wegely porcelain factory, Berlin cup and saucer. c.1750–5 E

A late 18thC Berlin tea caddy, painted in grisaille after Tenier. 4in (10cm) high F

Wegely also made small, Classical figures of the seasons on high, square pedestals. Although many examples are left in the white, some are painted with solid washes in which puce, iron red, and black tend to predominate.

Gotzkowsky's paste and glaze

The paste remained virtually the same at Gotzkowsky's factory until about 1770, when new materials were employed. These produced a colder-looking paste with a greyish tone to it. The glaze was also colder than before and had a more bluish tone to it.

Gotzkowsky's wares

A KPM Berlin vase and cover. c.1800 11.75in (30cm) high F

Some of the finest Berlin porcelains were made with this new clay between 1770 and 1786. The factory transformed Meissen and Sèvres models thereby creating and developing a delicate, late Rococo style of its own. This style employed a shallow moulded decoration with a scaled pattern, moulded rims, and hesitant gilding.

Gotzkowsky's figures

Friedrich and Wilhelm Meyer produced the best and most famous series of Berlin figures during Gotzkowsky's ownership. This included the Cries of Berlin. The brothers also made a number of Classical figures, usually with allegorical themes. These figures are often elongated and have relatively small heads. The figures were characteristically painted in

- black
  - pale salmon pink
    - puce.

Apart from the early Rococo bases, most of Gotzkowsky's figures are mounted on simple, square-shaped slabs. In common with Vienna, Paris, and Derby, Berlin used the porcelain as a vehicle for miniature painting. Entire plates were covered with similar enamelling

A 19thC KPM Berlin cup and saucer. G

A KPM Berlin coffee set, with bright and matt gilt "Neuzierat" decoration. 1849–70 coffee pot 6.5in (16.5cm) high F

and gilding, which often makes it impossible to identify the factory by its style or its paste. The Berlin factory continued to make high-quality decorated porcelain until the end of the 19thC. Most of the porcelain displays Classical influences. Berlin's tradition of creating porcelain as a medium for painting reached its high point from c.1840 with the development of porcelain plaques.

Marks

Wegely's mark is an underglaze or impressed "W", sometimes accompanied by fractional numbers representing the type of paste and series numbers of the moulds. Gotzkowsky's marks included a "G", a sceptre taken from the arms of Brandenburg, or the Hapsburg eagle over the initials "KPM":

- when this is red, it represents 1823–32
- when this is blue and red it represents the period 1832–44
- when it is only blue, it represents from 1844 onwards
- from 1832, an orb over the initials "KPM" was also used.

A KPM Berlin cup and saucer, with the coat of arms of the von Reichel family. 1849–70 Cup 3.25in (8cm) high G

Zürich

A Zürich cup and saucer, with landscapes. 1765–90 H

1. Is the glaze greyish or smoky cream?
2. If the piece is a figure, is it slightly stiffly moulded?
3. Is the figure painted in broad washes and rather pale pastel colours?
4. Is the base of the figure moulded as simple rockwork or a mossy mound?
5. If the piece is a ware, is it decorated with a particularly fine landscape vignette?
6. Are the leaves on the trees in the landscape a greyish green and finely detailed in black or brown?

Zürich (1763–1897)

The most important factory in Switzerland was founded by the artist Salomon Gessner at Scoren in 1763, under the direction of A. Spengler.

Paste and glaze

The factory first made a soft-paste, then a hard-paste around 1765. This paste has a greyish, granular body, which sometimes fires a reddish or brownish

A Zürich plate, painted with a boat and figures in a river landscape. c.1770 9in (23cm) diam H

colour. The glaze is glassy, greyish, or smoky cream but can sometimes be rough and crumbly.

Wares

Domestic wares from Zürich are German Rococo or Neo-classical in style. Some of the wares have ribbing and puce floral decoration. Cups are tall with loop or wishbone handles. Teapots are usually bullet-shaped with flush lids and bud knops.

Landscapes

Salomon Gessner designed and painted the high-quality decoration on many of the wares himself. These were often soft landscapes and pastoral scenes in vignettes. Heinrich Thomann and Heinrich Fuseli created similar scenes after Anton Waterloo. The dominant early colours are:

- soft russet
- sky blue
- puce
- greyish yellow
- manganese
- purple.

In the 1780s two brighter colours were added:

- a stronger russet
- lemon yellow.

Figures

J. V. Sonnenschein made some very attractive if static figures in the late 1770s, reminiscent of Ludwigsburg.

Mark

The mark is a "Z" in underglaze blue with a horizontal line through its mid-point accompanied by a number of dots.

A early Zürich plate, with feather edge moulding. 9.5in (24cm) diam H

Saint-Cloud

A Saint-Cloud tea bowl and trembleuse *saucer.*
1710–20 Cup 5.5in (14cm) high F

1. Is the porcelain soft-paste
2. Is the glaze quite glassy?
3. Are there black flecks in the surface of the piece?
4. If it is polychrome, is it decorated in the Kakiemon style?
5. Are any handles very thick?
6. Does the underglaze blue decoration resemble miniature wrought ironwork?

Saint-Cloud (1664–1766)

The earliest recorded attempt to manufacture porcelain in France was in 1664, when Claude and François Reverend were granted the right to set up a factory at Saint-Cloud between Paris and Versailles. However, there are no extant examples which can be ascribed to a date before the 1690s. Martin Lister, an English doctor, visited the factory in 1698 and wrote that the director, François de Morin, had only recently perfected his porcelain after experimenting for 25 years. Lister said he could discern no difference between Saint-Cloud porcelain and Chinese porcelain, except that he felt Saint-Cloud's decoration was more accomplished than the Oriental.

An early 18thC Saint-Cloud cane handle.
1.75in (4.5cm) high H

Wares

Saint-Cloud produced a large range of domestic wares. Some of these domestic wares included:

• circular soup tureens and covers
• teapots with dragon or bird's neck handles and spouts
• elaborate figurative or bird-shaped jugs
• chinoiserie pot-pourri encrusted with flowers and supported on rockwork bases
• trefoil spice boxes raised on small legs

A Saint-Cloud table salt. 1710–20
2.25in (6cm) wide F

An early 18thC Saint-Cloud Kakiemon crow's beak cane handle. E

87

- flower-encrusted baskets
- handles for canes and knives
- salts in "waisted" capstan or chamfered rectangular shapes
- cylindrical pots
- cups and saucers, butter dishes, jam pots, and cruet stands
- snuff boxes
- ice pails.

The curving handles on pots, jugs, and cups are always thick and either grooved or slab-sided, often in the form of dragons and other animals.

- On larger vessels, the handles are modelled in the form of monstrous, gaping animal masks.

Decoration

On early pieces, such as the tea bowl and saucer (see p.86), the underglaze blue decoration often looks like wrought ironwork in the style of the French Baroque.

- From c.1730 onwards, polychrome enamelling follows the fashion for Kakiemon, but it is primitive and stiff and the colours are nothing like the Japanese palette.

- Due to the sumptuary laws (see p. 102) there is little gilding.

Palette

The dominant colours are:
- dirty, egg-yolk yellow

A Saint-Cloud porcelain box, modelled with a hunter and his dog. c.1740 2.75in (7cm) wide G

- yellowish green
- turquoise
- sky blue
- blood red
- black.

A feature of many early Saint-Cloud wares is prunus moulding based on Chinese motifs. However, the flowers tend to be more realistic than the stylized Chinese versions, with sharper, more delicate detailing than on the heavily glazed Chinese originals. Other mouldings include wading birds and overlapping leaves, like the surface of an artichoke.

Paste and glaze

Saint-Cloud soft-paste uses a fine, greyish-white paste, often with tiny black flecks. The glaze is creamy white with hints of olive green where it has pooled. It is less shiny than the Mennecy glaze and gives a warm satin-like sheen. This *bonbonnière*, modelled as a hunter, is typical of the small pieces made at Saint-Cloud in the mid-18thC. Less than 3in (7.5cm) tall, it is decorated with delicate flowers in the Kakiemon palette and is, typically, mounted on silver. The French control marks on the silver help to date these pieces.

A Saint-Cloud white-glazed box with lid, moulded with branches of flowering prunus. c.1740–5 2.25in (6cm) wide F

Figures

Figures made by Saint-Cloud in the earlier 18thC (mainly chinoiserie) are usually more finely detailed. Most are in white, with nothing to distract from their crisp modelling. Elaborate pot-pourri vases became a speciality of the factory in the middle of the 18thC. They are usually in the white, almost always encrusted with flowers, and often set on moulded rockwork bases.

Marks

The most common Saint-Cloud mark is an incised "St C" over a "T" standing for the Trou family, which acquired the factory by marriage at the end of the 17thC. Another quite common mark is a painted sun with a face on it.

A Saint-Cloud Chinese figure. c.1740 8in (20.5cm) high H

Chantilly

A Chantilly Kakiemon magot, with bronze mounts. c.1740 12.5in (32cm) wide AA

1. Is the piece soft-paste?
2. Is the glaze creamy and opaque?
3. If the piece is a figure, does it have chinoiserie decoration?
4. Is the modelling of any figures indistinct and lacking in detail, particularly on the face and hands?
5. If enamelled, do the colours reflect the typical Kakiemon palette (see opposite), and are they painstakingly outlined in black?
6. If not enamelled, does the piece have a white body painted in underglaze blue or in conventional Rococo colours dominated by puce and brown?
7. Does the decoration have a stiff linear quality, and show signs of detailed brushwork?

Chantilly
(c.1725–1800)

The factory was established c.1725 under the patronage of the Prince of Condé, an avid collector of Kakiemon, and produced a wide range of useful and decorative wares, which typically included:

A pair of Chantilly Kakiemon wine coolers. c.1735–40 6.25in (16cm) high AA

- figures; almost all of which are Oriental in style and often seen reclining beside large baluster pot-pourri jars
- bough pots
- jardinières or cachepots
- teapots
- beakers
- small écuelles or sauce tureens
- plates
- hot water jugs
- coffee pots.

The pair of *seau à bouteille* above are typical of the simpler line of the 1730s, which 20 or so years later was to give way to the sinuous curves of the Rococo. They are decorated in typical Japanese Kakiemon colours of iron-red, turquoise, blue, yellow, and dark manganese. The emphasis on flower-based motifs is characteristically Japanese, a style for which Chantilly is famous. The thin handles are typical, but Chantilly also used dragon and human face forms, like Saint-Cloud.

Some similarities between the products of Chantilly and Saint-Cloud are not surprising as the manager, Ciquaire Cirou, had worked at both establishments.

A Chantilly white-glazed bouquetière figure. c.1735–40 9.75in (25cm) high E

A Chantilly Kakiemon crow's beak cane handle. c.1735–40 3in (7.5cm) long F

This mark c.1725–89

*A Chantilly
custard cup and
cover. c.1740
3in (7.5cm)
high H*

Mid- to late 18thC wares

Following the death of the Prince of
Conde in 1740, the factory became less
ambitious and more fashion lead.
Kakiemon style, beloved by the Prince,
gave way to the sprays of *deutsche
Blumen* – in vogue at many French
factories as well as at Meissen. The
Chantilly interpretation was much
looser than the rather academic
treatment at the German factory.
By the 1760s, the flamboyant
Rococo wares of Sèvres
had become a major
source of inspiration,
although Chantilly
was forbidden by the
royal monopoly to
employ gilding. This
factory is well known
for its blue and white

*A Chantilly flower-decorated
plate. c.1760
5in (12.5cm) diam H*

porcelains, such as the "Chantilly Sprig"
seen on this custard cup and cover
(see left). By c.1780 the factory was in
decline and was closed in 1800.

Identification points

Like Chantilly, Meissen outlined
their colours in black. However, their
porcelain has a cold, glassy translucent
glaze, whereas that of Chantilly is
distinctively creamy and opaque –
the result of adding tin to conceal
imperfections. Most wares are under
10in (25.5cm) tall, probably because
above that size soft-paste pieces tended
to sag or collapse in the kiln. On larger
items, look out for cracks, splits, or tears,
sometimes obscured by the decoration.

Kakiemon-style wares

Many items were close copies of
Kakiemon wares, both in form and
decoration. It is probably that such
pieces were copied directly from
specimens in the personal
collection of the Prince
of Condé. The figure
on p.90, is typical of
Chantilly Kakiemon
in a number of ways:
• The patterns
have a flat, linear
appearance,
common to many
Kakiemon-type
wares, as the enamels
tended to sink into the

glaze. However, the use of black outlining helps to distinguish wares both from the more painterly style of true Japanese enamelling and from the Kakiemon wares made by other French porcelain factories during the early 18thC, such as Saint-Cloud and Mennecy.

• The brushwork is highly detailed, especially on the robes, which are decorated with scattered flowers.

• The distinct lack of detailed modelling, particularly in the face and on the hands, is typical of the factory's early soft-paste figures. The inclusion of a vase is typical. Like all European attempts at the Oriental, the facial features are somewhat unconvincing.

• The form, which is linear and almost triangular, is weighted at the base to support the figure.

Marks

All wares carry the Chantilly mark of a small hunting horn. This was red

A pair of Chantilly Kakiemon ormolu-mounted incense burners. c.1780 D

until c.1750 and thereafter in a less distinct underglaze blue, or occasionally in other colours, especially red or manganese. A letter sometimes appears under the horn. This may represent the initial letter of the name of the factory's proprietor during the period when the piece was made.

Copies

Beware of imitations by the Paris firm, Samson. These were not originally intended to deceive, but quite often their mark – a pair of tiny entwined "S"s – has been removed. Examine the glaze: Samson wares invariably employ a glassy hard-paste porcelain that is very different from the less lustrous soft-paste used by Chantilly.

A mid-18thC Chantilly quatrefoil sucrier, cover, and stand. F

Mennecy

A mid-18thC Mennecy teapot and cover. 6in (15.5cm) high F

1. Is the porcelain soft-paste?
2. Is the glaze creamy, glassy, and translucent?
3. Is the piece quite small?
4. If the piece is a figure, does it have a pyramid shape?
5. Does the figure have any splits or tears?
6. Is it leaning back and looking upwards?
7. Is it thickly constructed?
8. Are the colours on the figure loose and washed out?
9. If the piece is a small vessel, is it rimmed in puce?
10. If the piece is a cup, is it shaped like a bell or a bucket?

Mennecy (1734–80)

Established in 1734 by François Barbin, under the Duc de Villeroy, production was moved from Paris to Mennecy. In 1766, the factory was then bought by the sculptor Joseph Jullien and the painter Charles-Symphorien Jacques. By 1773, however, the factory had moved to Bourg-la-Reine. After 1780 the factory only produced creamware.

Wares

Mennecy's paste is mellow and ivory-coloured. The glaze is creamy white, glassy, and translucent; wares tend to be small, but have a style of their own. Mennecy figures are rare and heavy-looking, with splits or tears. Teapots are similar to the Vincennes or Sèvres style with ovoid bodies, domed covers, and ear-shaped handles. Mennecy cups are, on the whole, plain-sided with wishbone, strap handles. There are relatively few plates. This custard pot (see above) has the moulded spiral

A Mennecy custard cup and cover c.1765 3.5in (9cm) high G

and vertical fluting that was regularly used to break up the shapes. After 1740 the Rococo style was brought in, which was dominated by puce or pink. Other colours were:

- rich egg-yolk
- pale daffodil
- deep sky blue
- greyish turquoise
- green.

Marks

The Mennecy mark is the letters "DV". This stands for the Duc de Villeroy. Sometimes this mark is painted but usually it is incised.

A mid-18thC Mennecy cup and saucer, painted with colourful birds. G

A Mennecy monkey's head snuff box. c.1755 2.25in (6cm) wide H

Vincennes and early Sèvres

*A Vincennes jug,
painted with a
gilt-edged cartouche
of birds. c.1750
4.5in (11.5cm) high E*

1. Is the porcelain soft-paste?
2. Is the glaze glassy and translucent?
3. Does the enamel appear to sink into the glaze?
4. Is any gilding thick, so that it is easy to feel, and tooled, that is, detailed with lines or other embellishment?
5. If the piece is a figure, is it heavy and pyramid-shaped?
6. Is the piece marked with two interlaced "Ls", possibly incorporating a date letter?
7. Is there an additional mark, either initials or a device?

Vincennes and early Sèvres (1738–59)

Vincennes was established as a soft-paste factory in 1738, with the help of craftsmen from Chantilly. Vincennes became the national porcelain factory of France and stylistically one of the most influential in mid-18thC Europe. Although it was at first unsuccessful, its future was secured in 1745, when it was granted a 20-year monopoly to make porcelain in the style of Meissen.

The move to Sèvres

In 1756, the Vincennes factory moved from its original site to the château of Sèvres, near the home of King Louis XV's mistress, Madame de Pompadour, and it was through her influence that the King became sole owner in 1759. In 1769, when a suitable clay was found in France, Sèvres gradually switched to producing hard-paste, and c.1803 finally abandoned the most successful soft-paste formula ever used. The shape, the heavy handles,

A Vincennes sugar bowl and cover, gilt with exotic birds. c.1753 3.5in (9cm) high E

and the Meissen-style puce landscape decoration of this wine glass cooler (see below left), made c.1750–2, show the strong influence of the German factory in the first stages at Vincennes. By 1753, this style had been replaced by Rococo shapes with flutes and wavy rims.

Wares

The factory concentrated on making bowls, pot-pourri vases, tea sets, and dinner services. The earliest wares

A Vincennes glass cooler, painted in the manner of Meissen in puce camaïeu. c.1750–2 5.25in (13cm) high C

A Vincennes pot-pourri. c.1750 5.5in (14cm) high F

are entirely derivative but in the 1740s Vincennes broke away from the Meissen tradition and developed the exuberant and individual style for which it was to become famous. Leading artists, including the goldsmith Jean-Claude Duplessis and the painter François Boucher, were employed to design the shapes and the decorations. Many of the sumptuous Rococo wares reflect the influence of metalwork but the results are not always harmonious. At times the handles and other appendages look a bit bolted on. Nevertheless, the factory became so successful that its influence can be seen in the products of most of the other European factories, including, ironically, Meissen.

A Vincennes 'pot à boire', for the Turkish market. 1755 8.75in (22cm) high AAA

Decoration

Vincennes and early Sèvres glaze is glassy and translucent, even more than other soft-pastes. The warm, lustrous surface is highly receptive to enamelling, which sinks in and merges with it.

• The most popular themes include landscapes, figures, birds, and flowers.
• The brushwork is generally freer than on the hard-paste porcelain from the German factories.

Ground colours

During the Rococo period a series of brilliant ground colours were introduced to serve as a backcloth to the representational panels. The factory is as well known for its sumptuous ground colours as its painting, such as from

• 1749, *bleu lapis* – a rich, almost purple cobalt blue
• 1752, *bleu celeste* – sky blue
• 1753, *jaune jonquille* – a pale lemon yellow
• 1756, *vert pomme* – mid-green
• 1757, *violette* – violet
• 1758, rose pink, later incorrectly known as *rose Pompadour*
• 1763, *bleu royal* – a rich enamel blue.

Gilding

The brilliant colours are enhanced by the finest tooled gilding on any porcelain, except for the work on some of Chelsea's

A Vincennes bleu celeste cup and saucer, with flowers. 1754 Saucer 3.75in (9.5cm) diam E

A Sèvres stand, painted with four gilt shell-shaped "C" scrolls. 1761 7in (18cm) long E

porcelain from the gold-anchor period (1758–68). Almost all other gilding seems flat by comparison.

Because of the sumptuary laws (see p.102), other French factories substituted gilding with blue or purple border decoration.

Marks

The pre-revolution marks on Vincennes and early Sèvres pieces are interlaced "L"s (the cipher of Louis XV), which first appeared in underglaze blue in the 1740s. In 1753 date letters were introduced (appearing in the space between the "L"s), starting with "A" for 1753 and continuing through to "Z" for 1777. The year 1778 was then designated by a pair of "A"s, and so on. In addition, artists signed their work with their own cipher or device. This was

This mark "I" for 1761

usually initials, but occasionally it was a pictogram such as the running fox of Emile Renard.

Copies

It is important to remember that the interlaced "L"s of Vincennes and early Sèvres, together with the crossed swords of Meissen, are by far the most copied marks on European porcelain. Probably more than 90 per cent of the interlaced "L"s are on later hard-paste copies made in Paris or Limoges. However, relatively few copies have date letters between the "L"s. The Vincennes and early Sèvres factory made a handful of figures and groups in unglazed biscuit and occasionally glazed porcelain. The production of these, however, was very limited compared to wares. The extreme plasticity of the soft-paste meant that figures wilted or collapsed in the heat of the oven.

A Sèvres two-handled cup, cover, and stand. 1761. 7.5in (19cm) wide F

Royal Sèvres

A Sèvres cup and saucer, painted by Charles-Nicolas Dodin. c.1778 Cup 3in (7.5cm) high D

1. Is the quality of the gilding exceptional?
2. Is the piece decorated with an identifiable coloured ground (see p.98), or with a patterned ground?
3. If the piece is a vessel, does it serve both a practical and a decorative purpose?
4. Have the enamels sunk into the glaze?
6. If the piece is a dish or a basin, are the edges lobed?
7. Is the piece decorated with flowers or cartouches of putti amid clouds? (But beware Meissen and Derby copies.)
8. Is the mark right (see p.99)?

Sèvres (1756–c.1780)

The quality of Sèvres porcelain cannot be overstated. Each piece is a work of art and many are unsurpassed wonders of ceramic production. Once a piece of the finest Sèvres porcelain is seen it is not forgotten. The rich ground colours or decorations, meticulous painting, and tooled gilding when combined with its inventive shapes have rarely been surpassed. Royal patronage was always important and from 1759 the factory became the Manufacture Royale de Sèvres, fully owned by King Louis XV. The support of the King, his mistress, and courtiers was key to the success of the factory. To this day it is still owned by the French State. In many ways the products were playthings of the Ancien Régime. In the years

A Sèvres teapot and cover, with blue and gilt oeil de perdrix *ground. c.1775 4.25in (11cm) high F*

immediately before and after the move from Vincennes to Sèvres, the French royal porcelain factory made its most complex pieces. During the 1750s and 1760s it employed many of France's finest artists, not only designers and painters but also sculptors, bronze-founders, and goldsmiths. Principal among these was the Royal Goldsmith Giovanni Claudio Ciambellano, better known by his French name of Jean-Claude Duplessis, who created new shapes never before seen in porcelain between 1747 and 1774. François Boucher, who later became first painter to the King, also created shapes for the works. High artistry was combined with rigorous quality control that saw any piece with the slightest warping, pitting, or discoloration rejected. Despite this control, many of these "seconds" were somehow smuggled out of the factory and decorated in other

A Sèvres cup and saucer, from the Catherine II of Russia service. 1778–9 3.Cup 25in (8cm) high D

A Sèvres tray, decorated with flowers on a bleu céleste ground. 1780 9in (23cm) diam E

workshops, mainly in Paris. These are never the same quality, however, and it is unlikely that any of them could be mistaken for genuine Sèvres. In order to protect his commercial interests, King Louis XV enacted sumptuary laws, which prohibited any other French factory or workshop from using gilding or enamelling. The gilding at this period was mixed using honey, which gives it a softer, more yellow look.

Range of products

The French used a larger range of tablewares than any other nation, and in the second half of the 18thC the range of wares at Sèvres was correspondingly large. In addition, the factory made pieces that combined a useful and a decorative purpose, such as a pot-pourri and a vase. But it also made decorated biscuit figures, clock cases, and plaques. These plaques were inset in the elaborate furniture of Martin Carlin and Bernard Van Reisenburgh. The factory continued to produce realistic models of flowers that had first been made at Vincennes. These were often bought by middlemen known as *marchand-merciers* and were mounted on painted metal stems for display in vases or to add to elaborate ormolu settings for Meissen figures, in the same way as *bocage* was later used in England. In the late 1760s, Sèvres introduced a number of patterned grounds, such as caillouté (pebbled) (see jug p.96) and *oeil de perdrix* (partridge eye), which was used on the teapot (see p.101).

• The trophies in reserve panels was a favourite theme of around 1770. Some were painted by Pierre-Antoine Méreaud and Charles Buteux, whose relatives were also employed as decorators at the Sèvres factory.

• Pear-shaped ewers were made at many 18thC factories, but the Sèvres version certainly has the most elegantly proportioned shape.

A Sèvres tureen, cover, and stand, painted by Borleau. 1785 6.25in (16cm) diam D

A Sèvres covered sugar bowl, painted by Claude-Antoine Tardy. c.1780 4.25in (11cm) high E

A Sèvres teapot, painted by Tentard. 1780 5in (12.5cm) high E

• Oval basins were also common, but only Sèvres embellished the line of the edges with lobes.

The Sèvres factory was the pioneer of "biscuit" (unglazed and undecorated) figures and groups. Without any decorative coating, the models are much crisper, and as the porcelain in this state resembles marble, it became a particularly popular medium for Neo-classical figures. The fashion for biscuit is said to have started when Madame de Pompadour visited the factory to see the progress of some figures. She admired the unfinished models so much that she ordered them to be delivered as they were. Many examples were created by the great sculptor Etienne-Maurice Falconet, who worked as chief modeller at the factory from 1757 to 1766 and often based his models on his own statues. Falconet would sometimes also use prints by the leading French Rococo painter, François Boucher, who designed decorations for the Royal Sèvres factory.

A Sèvres écuelle, cover, and stand, decorated with chinoiserie garden scenes. c.1783 D

Post-Revolutionary Sèvres

A Sèvres imperial porcelain pot-pourri canopic jar, with a pharaoh's head on the lid. 1804–9 11in (28cm) high E

1. Is the porcelain hard-paste? (Soft-paste was used occasionally until c.1800.)
2. If visible, is the porcelain body pure white?
3. Are the paste and glaze flawless?
4. Is the gilding very high quality?
5. Is the mark right (see opposite and pp.216–17)?

Sèvres (c.1780–1810)

During the 1770s and 1780s the principal style became more Neo-classical. After the French Revolution the factory was taken over by the State and production nearly came to a standstill. A considerable quantity of porcelain blanks were sold off, many of which were purchased by English factories and decorators.

Alexander Brongniart

Sèvres was saved from extinction in 1800, when Alexander Brongniart was appointed director. He reorganized the operation of the factory, abandoned the production of soft-paste, and invented a new hard-paste, which is close-grained, snow-white, and looks like perfect icing (frosting). This new paste took solid ground colours more effectively. Brongniart also developed a range of rich new enamel colours, which gave

A pair of early 19thC Sèvres ormolu-mounted vases. 22.5in (57cm) high D

A Sèvres First Empire swan cup and saucer, with gilt interior. 1804–14 2.5in (6.5cm) high F

the decorations the deep tone of oil paintings, and a new glaze, which is slightly grey, but also clear, flawless, glassy, and translucent. During the mid-19thC the factory began copying the works of well-known contemporary artists onto porcelain, Brongniart's new colours being ideal for this purpose. Until about 1850, the factory still espoused Classical forms and decoration. Dark blue is a much more common ground colour in this period.

Marks

From 1793 until 1804, Sèvres porcelain is marked "RF" for République Française in underglaze blue. Between 1800 and 1802, the word "Sèvres" appears alone, either in gold or in colours. In 1803–5 the letters "M. N le Sèvres" – manufacture Nationale le Sèvres – were used. This mark was in red.

Paris

An early 19thC pair of Jacob Petit vases. 21in (53cm) high D

1. Is the porcelain hard-paste, pure white, and flawless?
2. Is the glaze hard and glassy?
3. Does the enamelling sit on the surface of the paste?
4. Is the gilding worn away in places?
5. If the piece is a large vessel, does it have a flared rim?
6. If the piece is a plate, does it have a spur mark in the centre of the base?
7. If the piece is a figure, is it biscuit?
8. Is there a cursive incised mark on the base?

The Paris factories

Following the discovery of china clay in the Limousin region of France in the 1770s a large number of high-quality hard-paste factories were established in Paris. Despite the laws established by Louis XV forbidding the use of gold and enamels, many firms copied the work of the royal factory. Most simply ignored the law, while others sought patronage of members of the royal family, hoping that this would allow them to continue production unhindered. One of the earliest successful Paris factories was the Rue Thiroux factory established in 1776 by André-Marie Leboeuf. His products quickly found success, followed by massive fines from Sèvres. Undaunted, Leboeuf sought the protective patronage of queen Marie Antoinette and his works became

A pair of mid-19thC Jacob Petit figural scent bottles, modelled as a sultan and Sultana. 11.75in (30cm) high E

known as the "Fabrique de la Reine". The Queen allowed the product to be marked with a capital "A". Following many protests, however, the sumptuary laws were relaxed, just before the 1789 Revolution.

An early 19thC Jacob Petit clock garniture. Clock 16.25in (41cm) high D

A Jacob Petit floral encrusted porcelain mantel clock. c.1870 16in (40.5cm) wide G

This mark c.1830–60

With the relaxation of the laws protecting Sèvres and the disarray at the royal factory following the Revolution, many Paris firms capitalized on the new market, creating rather severe-looking Neo-classical pieces more in tune with the times. These wares are characterized by highly burnished gilding with elaborate designs, often on coloured, matt grounds. The Paris hard-paste was very resistant to both enamelling and gilt. The decorations seem to sit on the surface and give no sense of having sunk in and become part of the paste, and on most pieces today there are patches where the gilding has worn away. The Paris factories were at their peak in the beginning of the 19thC, developing Neo-classical wares into Empire-style pieces for the Napoleonic era. Pot-bellied cups with flared rims,

A Paris vase, decorated in relief with masks and cupids. c.1830 22.5in (56.5cm) high D

An early 19thC P. L. Dagoty and E. Honoré part coffee service, painted with scenes of Paris. E

A pair of Darte Frères Paris porcelain vases, decorated with a Native American scene. c.1820 16.5in (42cm) high D

An early 19thC Dihl and Guérhard plate, with a horse carriage. 9.5in (24cm) diam D

high Grecian handles, and deep saucers are typical. As the rents and labour costs in Paris were higher than elsewhere and with the redevelopment of Paris by Baron Haussmann, by 1850 most factories had moved to Limoges, where production costs were lower and suitable clay was available nearby. Limoges has continued to be the main centre for the production of porcelain in France since.

Paste and glaze

Paris porcelain is a pure white, even, and virtually flawless hard-paste.

• The glaze is hard and glassy and rather unsympathetic-looking.

• In overall appearance, this white porcelain looks very similar to Nantgarw and Swansea. Many Paris wares were decorated outside the factories This P. L. Dagoty and E. Honoré example (see opposite right) is typical. Paris coffee pots often have spouts shaped like the heads of birds or animals, usually ducks or dragons. Like many pieces made by the Paris factories, the cups have flared rims and the handles are higher than the rims. The matt ground (in

A mid-19thC Feuillet plate. 9in (23cm) diam H

*A pair of P. D. Honoré pot-pourri vases. c.1860
9in (23cm) high E*

somewhat drab colours) and lavish use of highly burnished gilding is typical. This service is also typical of the combination of severe Neo-classical shapes, which, whenever possible, followed the form of Greek and Etruscan originals, and sensitive and highly accomplished contemporary designs, which usually showed hunting scenes, children at play, or, as here, named views of contemporary France.

Most Paris plates were fired on a spur and have a tiny mark on the base. Paris plates made between the end of the Revolution and 1830 generally have plain rims. However, during the next ten years some wares began to show the first signs of a Rococo revival. The Feuillet plate (see p.109) is typical of the later, more generically French style favoured by many of the later Paris factories. The

*A La Courtille Paris flared cabinet cup and saucer, in
Empire style. c.1820 4.75in (12cm) high G*

An early 19thC Locré plate, with a praying soldier. 9.5in (24cm) diam E

shallow moulding, gilding, and floral reserves could be 18thC Sèvres, but the naturalistic fruit decoration is typically 19thC. A leading figure in the movement back to Rococo was Jacob Petit. Born in Paris in 1792, Jacob Marddouche, who took his wife's surname of Petit, studied painting and worked for a brief period at Sèvres. He opened a small workshop in Belleville, then in 1833 bought the Baruch Weil factory at Fontainebleau, which soon saw royal patronage. Jacob Petit's productions were lavish and in tune with the times. Clock cases in the Neo-Rococo or Gothic style, with bright green, turquoise, or rich claret grounds, lavish gilding, and handmade flowers are typical, as is the use of new and inventive shapes. Vases with cabriole legs that are set on decorative bases, cornucopia, perfume burners, and figural paperweights are often seen with a prominent mark in blue "J.P." The gilding on these objects was rich, often raised, and has a spidery look to it.

An early 19thC Nast coffee pot and cover. 5in (12.5cm) high H

*Locré factory
This mark
c.1773–1830*

Tournai

A Tournai teapot and cover, from the Duc d'Orléans service. c.1787 4.75in (12cm) high C

1. Is the porcelain soft-paste?
2. Is the glaze warm with an ivory or grey tinge?
3. If a ware, is it moulded with fine spiral ribs?
4. Is the ware painted *en camaïeu*?
5. If the piece is a figure, is it biscuit or has it been left in the white? (Enamels are rare.)
6. Is the base rockwork?
7. Is the subject romantic?
8. Is the mark right (see opposite)?

An 18thC Tournai dish. 17.25in (44cm) wide F

Tournai, (1751–c.1850)

Founded by F. J. Peterinck, Tournai was the most important factory in the Low Countries, producing soft-paste porcelain from 1753.

Paste and glaze

Slightly off-white at first, it later became ivory-coloured and warmer. The glaze is soft, translucent, and mildly glassy.

Wares

The factory began by imitating Meissen and later, Sèvres. The most characteristic pieces are moulded with spiral panels and basketwork edges, or with very fine spiral ribs, similar

An 18thC Tournai dish. 10.5in (26.5cm) wide H

to those on Mennecy wares.

Decoration

Tournai decorated many wares with exotic bird patterns, similar to those used at Chelsea and Worcester, or in underglaze blue and overglaze *camaïeu* in rose or puce. Almost all Tournai wares, like these plates, are decorated with vignettes as opposed to framed panels. Many Tournai wares were sold in the white and decorated at The Hague, where they were usually enamelled with a stork mark. Although Tournai was at this time ruled by France, it was able to use gilding in defiance of the sumptuary laws (see p.102), due to the powerful patronage of the Austrian archduchess, Maria Theresa.

Figures

Tournai made a wide range of mainly contemporary figures and groups, in the white or in biscuit. These figures were often on tall rockwork bases with tree-stump supports.

Marks

The early factory mark is a tower in blue, crimson, or gold, or sometimes other colours. From c.1765, the mark was clumsily painted crossed swords with crosses in the angles.

113

Venice

A late 18thC Cozzi figure of a couple.
5in (12.5cm) high F

Cozzi

1. Does the piece look greyish?
2. Is it marked with a clumsy red anchor?
3. Do the handles or the spouts look eccentric?
4. Is the palette dominated by iron red, puce, and iridescent green?

Vezzi

1. Is the piece heavily potted?
2. Is the decoration applied or moulded?
3. Is there a noticeable wreathing in the body?
4. Is the glaze brownish where it has pooled?

Cozzi (1764–1812)

The most successful
Venetian factory
was opened by
Geminiano Cozzi.

Paste and glaze

The paste is greyish
and is covered in a
thin watery glaze.
However, the
greyness is not
as intense as at Doccia.

*A late 18thC Cozzi
Imari preserve pot,
cover, stand,
and spoon.
5in (12.5cm)
high F*

Shapes

The shapes generally follow the
fashions of contemporary German
and French porcelain, but the
vessels usually have distinctive
handles and spouts.

Decoration

Applied flowers are common on
Cozzi wares, but the usual form of
decoration is painting, in which iron
red, puce, and a luscious iridescent
green predominate.

Cozzi figures

Cozzi produced a large range
of figures. This included
corpulent Meissen-style
pagoda figures, Commedia
dell'Arte characters, dwarves
modelled after the engravings
of Jacques Callot, and
pyramid-shaped groups.
Coffee cans and saucers
were most popular.

Cozzi marks

A clumsily drawn anchor in iron red, not
like that of Chelsea, which is smaller
and much neater.

Vezzi (1720–27)

Vezzi porcelain is rare. It is usually
thickly potted, with a translucent,
white to grey/ivory body. The glaze
is clear, but can have tiny bubbles.
Where the glaze has pooled it can be
brownish. Shapes are mainly after
Chinese or silver models. Stiff leaves,
blanc de Chine style, or gadrooning
are typical as is occasionally crude
paintwork, excepting the work of
Ludovico Ortolani.

Vezzi marks

The Vezzi mark is "Venezia" or
an abbreviation, such as "Ven:a",
incised or painted in underglaze
blue, red, or gold.

*A late 18thC Cozzi Commedia
dell'Arte candlestick group.
12.5in (32cm) high G*

Capodimonte and Buen Retiro

A Capodimonte écuelle and cover, painted by Giovanni Caselli. c.1750 7.5in (19cm) diam F

1. Is the porcelain pure white?
2. Is it translucent and very refined, like icing (confectioner's) sugar?
3. Is the glaze lustrous?
4. If a tea and coffee ware, is it very thinly potted?
5. Is the decoration stippled or drawn with extremely fine brushwork?
6. If a figure, is it a pyramid shape?
7. Are flesh tones rendered in a violet colour?
8. Does the base have an unglazed margin running around the bottom?

Capodimonte (1743–59)

The most famous Italian porcelain factory was founded by Charles III of Bourbon, King of Naples, who established it in the grounds of his palace at Capodimonte.

Buen Retiro (1760–1812)

When Charles III became king of Spain in 1759 he took the entire staff of his factory with him to Madrid, and in the following year opened a new factory in the palace of Buen Retiro. This factory concentrated on figures and was active until 1808. However, the quality of the fine soft-paste deteriorated towards the end of the 18thC, and in 1803 a hard-paste was introduced.

Paste and glaze

The paste is close-grained and very white, not unlike the *blanc de Chine* ware from Dehua in southern China. The porcelain is covered in a brilliant glaze with the hint of an ivory tone.

*A pair of Buen Retiro vases, with painted scenes of Watteau. c.1770
8.75in (22cm) high C*

Wares

The factory began by basing its wares on Meissen or Chinese examples, with moulded shapes and carefully painted floral designs.

Figures

Capodimonte produced some of the best soft-paste porcelain, especially those modelled by Giuseppe Gricci. Most are set on rockwork, mound, or simple slab bases, with unglazed margins around the sides where excess glaze has been wiped away before firing.

Marks

The usual mark, at both factories, is a fleur-de-lys, impressed, painted in gold, or crudely drawn in underglaze blue.

*A Capodimonte table casket.
12.25in (31cm) long H*

Doccia

*A Doccia figure of "Il Capitano",
from the Commedia dell'Arte.
c.1760–5 5.25in (13cm) high E*

1. Does the porcelain appear grey?
2. If the piece is a ware, is it moulded with relief figures?
3. If a large-scale ware, has it split in the firing?
4. Are wares decorated with transfer printing in underglaze blue, or with stencilling?
5. If the piece is a coloured figure with a scroll base, is the base vigorously moulded and detailed in puce?
6. Do figures and moulded decorations have unnaturally reddish flesh tones?
7. Is the mark convincing (see opposite)?

Doccia (1735–present)

The Doccia factory was founded by the Marchese Carlo Ginori in 1735 and is still producing porcelain today.

Paste and glaze

The early porcelain at Doccia was a type of greyish hard-paste. The characteristically thin glaze emphasizes the underlying greyness, making it easy to recognize. However, the tone can be confused with Vezzi porcelain, notably on pieces made during the first years, when Doccia had no mark.

Palette

In the 18thC and early 19thC, the most prominent colours were:

- puce
- iron red
- sky blue
- yellow
- green.

Wares

At the Doccia factory, the output was mainly useful wares, but also boxes and caskets moulded in shallow relief with Classical subjects. It was one of the few factories to use transfer

A Doccia oval dish, with silver-shaped rims, brightly painted in the "Tulipano" pattern. c.1765 10in (25.5cm)

printing in underglaze blue.

Figures

Doccia figures are mainly Classical subjects and often massively proportioned. They are crisply modelled with well-defined musculature and usually left in white.

Marks

The mark, introduced after Carlo Ginori's death in 1757, is a star. This star was either impressed or painted in red, blue, or gold. A crowned "N" was used on wares that copied Capodimonte.

A pair of Doccia wine-glass coolers. c.1760 6in (15.5cm) high E

A Doccia sauceboat, each side richly enamelled with a spray of brightly coloured Oriental flowers, unmarked. c.1760 6.75in (17cm) long G

Chelsea 1745–52

A Chelsea "Goat and Bee" jug.
c.1745–7 4in (11.2cm) high D

1. Is the porcelain soft-paste?
2. Are there any black "pinholes" on the base?
3. Have the bases of hollow vessels and dishes been ground down?
4. Is the piece shaped like silverware of the day?
5. Are the form and the decoration derived from Meissen?
6. Is the palette predominantly puce, brown, and a greenish turquoise (especially 1749–52)?
7. If a figure, is it hollow and smooth inside?
8. If a vessel, does the piece have chocolate-brown rims?
9. Is it marked?

The Chelsea factory (1745–52)

The only 18thC English factory to concentrate entirely on luxury porcelain was founded in London in 1745 by Nicholas Sprimont, a Huguenot silversmith from Liège. Because he was aiming his products at "the Quality and Gentry", he opened his factory in Chelsea, close to the fashionable Ranelagh pleasure gardens. The history of the factory divides into four periods, each identified by a different mark.

Incised triangle (1745–49)

The mark for the earliest period is an incised triangle, although a few of the first pieces are marked with a trident piercing a crown in underglaze blue.

A Chelsea raised-anchor tall beaker, with Ho Ho and Phoenix bird decoration. c.1748–50 3in (7.5cm) high D

The small-scale tablewares produced during this period were predominantly cream jugs, beakers, teapots, and salts. It was Sprimont who introduced the influence of the French Rococo into

A Chelsea white-glazed beaker and trembleuse *saucer, the beaker moulded with tea-plant sprays, the saucer with prunus. c.1747 5in (12.5cm) high E*

A Chelsea raised-anchor deep fluted dish, painted with two tigers playing. c.1752 5in (12.5cm) wide C

121

A Chelsea white-glazed tawny owl, raised-anchor period. c.1750 7.75in (19.5cm) high B

Raised-anchor (1749–52)

In 1749 Sprimont moved his factory to new premises and introduced a new mark, an anchor moulded in shallow relief on a small oval pad. With financial backing from Sir Everard Fawkener, who was secretary to the King's brother, the Duke of Cumberland, Chelsea embarked on a brief period of expansion which was to be its most successful commercially and artistically. It is not known whether these payments were made on behalf of the Duke himself. If this is so, they represent a very rare instance of royal support for an English porcelain company.

Although the silverware shapes continued, the main influence at Chelsea during the raised-anchor

English porcelain, and the undulating, asymmetrical shapes of these wares reflected the designs he had earlier created in silver. Crayfish salts were also made at Worcester and the Plymouth and Bristol factories.

Incised-triangle paste

The earliest Chelsea soft-paste is glassy and creamy, like early Saint-Cloud or Mennecy. The milk-white glaze is often unevenly applied. It contains a few black "pinholes", and there is sometimes a very narrow, unglazed margin around the base of the piece.

A Chelsea Kakiemon beaker and saucer. c.1748–52 Saucer 6in (15.5cm) diam F

A Chelsea silver-shaped dish, painted with flowers, insects, and a butterfly.
c.1748
10in (25.5cm) wide F

period was Meissen. Many of the Kakiemon shapes and patterns that Meissen had been producing since the 1730s were copied in a new formula soft-paste porcelain and decorated using an autumnal palette of puce, brown, and greenish turquoise, similar to the palette at Vincennes.

As on most raised-anchor vessels, the rim of the dish above is edged in dark chocolate brown. This was in imitation of Meissen's version of the Kakiemon style, but on the original the decoration had a practical purpose – the Japanese vessels were rimmed in iron glaze to stop them chipping.

The most original decorations on raised-anchor wares are the scenes from *Aesop's Fables*, which continued to be used in the red-anchor period (see pp.124–7). These decorations were probably all painted around 1755 by Jefferyes Hammett O'Neale, an artist who later came to work at Worcester.

Raised-anchor paste

The raised-anchor paste is less glassy than incised-triangle paste, and the milky glaze has a duller and more opaque look, not unlike faïence.

The bases on many wares are covered in an uneven glaze with numerous "pinholes" and a few grey spots in the surface. Some wares were very thickly potted, which often made them warp during firing. Like Japanese porcelain, Chelsea wares were fired on top of three porcelain spurs, usually on the footrim but occasionally on the base. As this allowed glaze to dribble over the foot, the footrims of hollow vessels and dishes were usually ground down after firing.

A Chelsea Kakiemon fluted bowl, with a scalloped rim, painted with a tiger and dragon.
c.1750 4in (10cm) wide E

Chelsea red anchor 1752–7

A pair of Chelsea large melon-shaped tureens and covers. c.1755 6.75in (17cm) wide A

1. Is the porcelain soft-paste?
2. Is the piece decorated in typical red-anchor enamels (see p.126)?
3. Does the glaze have a bluish tinge in places where it has pooled?
4. If the piece is shaped like a fruit or vegetable, is it meticulously modelled?
5. Are the wares decorated in the Meissen or Kakiemon style, or with large-scale botanical specimens?
6. If the piece is a figure, is the decoration very restrained?
7. Is the piece a miniature?
8. If a hollow figure, does it have a smooth interior?

A Chelsea pierced, oval two-handled basket. c.1756 11.25in (28.5cm) long F

Red-anchor (1752–7)

In 1752 the Chelsea mark changed to a small and neatly pencilled iron-red anchor, usually no more than ¼ in (5mm) in height. This mark continued until 1757 when Sprimont's illness caused the factory to be closed for over a year.

Red-anchor paste

At first red-anchor products were made in the raised-anchor paste, but after about 18 months Sprimont introduced a new formula that was more suited to the elaborate shapes that were then coming into fashion. The new porcelain is translucent and greenish when held to the light. The clear glaze often has a bluish tinge in places where it

This mark red-anchor period c.1752–7

has been too generously applied or has pooled in the angles.

The Meissen style continued to influence Chelsea wares until c.1757, when the more sumptuous Sèvres style began to take over. Like several English factories, Chelsea made baskets in

A Chelsea Kakiemon dish. c.1752–5 12.25in (31cm) diam E

simulated canework, but the detailed moulding and the painted and applied flowers on the Chelsea products are that of a much higher quality.

A Chelsea wine cooler, with Rococo-scroll side handles. c.1755 8in (20.5cm) high E

Tureens

It was during the red-anchor period of 1752–7 that Chelsea made its famous Rococo tureens in the shapes of fruit, vegetables, and animals. Although the artichoke shape of the tureens is unique to the Chelsea factory, many other vegetables, such as cauliflowers and melons, were also made at Worcester and Longton Hall, as well as a number of Continental factories. However, it is the Chelsea modelling and painting that stand out as the most meticulous. The most famous of all Chelsea's red-anchor products are the "Hans Sloane" wares – so called because their decorations were said to represent botanical specimens from Sir Hans Sloane's Chelsea Physic Garden and were based on engravings by the curator, Philip Miller, and Georg Dionysius Ehret. The specimens take up most of the surface of the wares and are painted in great detail and on a much larger scale than the flowers and plants on any other wares. Bow's botanical wares are generally of inferior workmanship.

• Many plates are populated by winged insects, bugs, and butterflies; and these, together with the plants, are often given shadowed outlines in the manner of J. G. Klinger of Meissen.

• The wine cooler above contains all the main colours of the red-anchor palette. Chelsea's red-anchor figures are influenced by Meissen, but lack movement, and the heavy glaze makes

A Chelsea creamboat, by Jefferyes Hammett O'Neale. c.1752–7 4in (10cm) wide B

them less severe. As can be seen from this figure of "Winter" (see right), modelled by Joseph Willems around 1755, the colouring is much more subdued than on figures from other English factories, and the features much more detailed.

Early red-anchor wares exhibit small patches of greater translucency, called "moons", when held to the light. The wares include some extremely well-modelled figures, nearly all of which were based on those of Johann Joachim Kändler and his assistants at Meissen. Especially notable are the Italian comedy figures, the characters represented in typical poses. Recently, some of the finest figures have been attributed to a Belgian modeller, Joseph Willems, and these include the 21in (53cm) "Una and the Lion," the largest figure made at Chelsea. The fashion for decorative table settings, of which the figures formed part, led to the making of large centrepieces, epergnes, and tureens in a variety of forms – rabbits, carp, twin doves, asparagus bundles, and cabbages – while dessert dishes were often modelled in leaf form. Flower-painting included imitations of Meissen *indianische Blumen* (Oriental flowers) and *deutsche Blumen* (naturally delineated German flowers).

A Chelsea figure of "Winter", modelled by Joseph Willems. c.1755 5.25in (13cm) high E

A Chelsea model of a sheep. c.1755 4in (10cm) high E

Chelsea gold anchor 1759–69

A Chelsea figure of a dancing man, gold anchor mark. c.1760 7.75in (19.5cm) high D

1. Is the porcelain soft-paste and comparatively opaque?
2. Is the glaze thick and bluish?
3. Does the glaze have a wide crackle?
4. Are wares extensively covered in high-quality gilding?
5. If the ground is dark blue or claret, is it very patchy?
6. If the piece is a figure, does it have a small head?
7. Is it very elaborately decorated?
8. Is it set on a symmetrical Rococo-scroll base?
9. Is the base enclosed (unlike early Chelsea)?

Gold anchor (1759–69)

In 1759, the Chelsea factory reopened with a new mark – a thick gold anchor – signifying a complete change. German restraint gave way to the French flamboyance of Sèvres.

Paste and glaze

The exuberant Rococo modelling was made possible by the use of a new paste formula, containing bone ash, which could be thickly potted and tended to result in heavier, more opaque wares. However, the advantages of the new paste were partly counteracted by the new glaze, which was thick and bluish.

Decoration

The designs on gold-anchor wares are painted in a bright palette. In most cases they are set against solid coloured grounds embellished with rich gilding.

Figures

Gold-anchor figures are as elaborate

A Chelsea cup and saucer. c.1765
Cup 6in (15.5cm) high E

as the wares. Most of them are inspired by prints. The technique of building up models with encrusted flowers and leaves, known as *bocage*, originated at Chelsea in this period. Although the device was later copied by most English factories, it was never used elsewhere in Europe.

Bases

Gold-anchor figures have high, pierced, scroll bases, heightened with gilding and encrusted with applied flowers.

A Chelsea saucer dish, painted in purple monochrome. c.1765 6.75in (17cm) diam F

This mark gold-anchor period 1759–69

A Chelsea vase, painted with exotic birds. c.1765
8in (20.5cm) high F

129

"Girl in a Swing"

*A "Girl in a swing" factory gilt-metal-mounted bonbonniere and
cover, modelled as a French hen sitting on her brood. 1749–54
2in (6cm) high D*

1. Is the paste "glassy" like Chelsea's but with a greater percentage
   of lead?
2. Does the "Girl-in-a-Swing" product appear to imitate Chelsea
   porcelain models?
3. Is the modelling crisp and well defined?
4. Is the piece decorated in polychrome, or left in the white?
5. Is it decorated with flowers?
6. Is the piece a "toy" – a perfume bottle, etui, or patch box?
7. If the piece is a scent bottle, does it have a gold or gilt-metal mount?

"Girl-in-a-Swing" factory (c.1748–59)

The so-called "Girl-in-a-Swing" group of porcelain figures, scent bottles, and wares were named after a specific figure of a girl in a swing, supported by two leafy trunks, which is in the Victoria and Albert Museum, London. The wares were originally attributed to the Chelsea factory of Nicholas Sprimont (1716–71). Recent research has proved that these figures and wares were made by Charles Gouyn (died 1785). Gouyn, a Huguenot born in Dieppe, was a second-generation jeweller with premises in St James's, London, and he had been a partner in the Chelsea factory until sometime before March 1749.

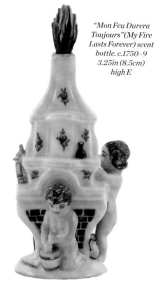

"Mon Feu Durera Toujours" (My Fire Lasts Forever) scent bottle. c.1750–9 3.25in (8.5cm) high E

However, the precise location of his factory, and the identity of the modeller of these distinctive figures, remains unknown.

The tiny figures, most of which are in the white, are wonderfully angular and unlike anything from figures made by any other English factory.

There are no marks that are associated with this factory.

A "Girl-in-a-Swing" triple scent bottle, modelled as four chickens, with gilt-metal mounts. c.1750–9 3in (7.5cm) high D

131

Bow

*A Bow cup, painted with exotic birds, insects, and a
caterpillar. c.1755–8. 5in (12.5cm) high F*

1. Is the paste white and chalky?
2. Is the glaze greenish and glassy?
3. Is the paste granular?
4. Does the piece display peppering – with spots on the paste?
5. If the piece is decorated in polychrome, do the colours include sky
   blue, egg-yolk yellow, and puce?
6. If the piece is a ware, is it decorated in an Oriental style?

Bow (1744–75)

Founded by Thomas Frye and Edward Heylyn in 1744, Bow was much less exclusive than the other great London factory, Chelsea. It made wares and figures for a much wider market, and grew to become the largest factory in England, but after 1760 it declined, and was finally sold off in 1775.

Paste and glaze

Bow paste is white and chalky with an open, granular texture and an irregular surface. The glaze is glassy, greyish, or greenish, and has a tendency to peppering or cracking.

Palette

Bow used many colours, but the three that dominated the palette in the mid-1750s were:
- milky, deep sky blue
- rich, egg-yolk yellow
- deep, purplish puce.

Wares

Almost all Bow wares were based on Oriental designs:
- Initial output consisted of two types: *blanc de Chine*-style wares, with the sides of vessels and dishes moulded in

A Bow teapot and cover, after a Japanese shape, painted in the famille rose *palette, with replacement handle.*
c.1753 6.25in (16cm) high E

shallow relief with pine, prunus, or bamboo.
- Underglaze blue designs were taken from both China and Japan. Even the later enamelled wares were based on *famille rose* or, more commonly, Kakiemon designs. The decoration of a European version of a *famille rose* pattern – was used at Bow between 1750 and 1760.

Marks

Bow used an anchor and dagger mark as well as other devices.

A Bow white-glazed model of a prowling lion. c1750 7.25in (18.5cm) wide D

Bow figures

A pair of Bow monkey sweetmeat dishes, modelled after Meissen. c.1758
5.5in (14cm) high C

1. If the piece is a figure, is it press-moulded and rather heavy?
2. Has the figure been left in the white (pre-1755)?
3. Has the thick glaze obscured some of the modelling?
4. Do the figures copy Meissen figures of the period?
5. Has the inspiration or decoration come from the Orient?
6. Do the figures represent famous theatrical personalities of the time?

Bow figures

Bow figures were press-moulded rather than slipcast. This gave them a heavier body, and in order to prevent them collapsing during firing, they were constructed almost architecturally. They were also covered in a heavy glaze, which tended to obscure the details.

A Bow porcelain figure of a girl playing a tambourine. c.1760 8.75in (22cm) high F

Most of the early Bow figures were left in the white. Many of the early figures are clumsily modelled.

By c.1755, the figures were well coloured in the characteristic Bow enamels. But they still stood on relatively simple mound bases, which were sometimes applied with flowers. However, after 1760 bases were moulded in the Rococo style and were often elevated on high scroll feet, like those in the figure above.

• Just as at Chelsea, the Bow modellers had a tendency to be over-elaborate and use overpowering tree-stump supports laden with blossom.

• Many of the later figures are relatively poorly modelled and far inferior to the Derby products of the same period.

An early Bow figure of "Matrimony", by the Muses modeller. c.1752–4 9.5in (24cm) high F

An 18thC Bow figure of a street cook. 6in (15.5cm) high F

First Period Worcester 1751–65

A Worcester cabbage-leaf jug, with the "Two Quails" pattern. c.1760–5 6.75in (17cm) high E

1. Is the paste greenish in transmitted light?
2. Are there isolated areas containing tiny, peppery pinpricks?
3. Is there an unglazed margin inside the footrim?
4. Is the piece moulded?
5. Is it decorated with underglaze transfer printing?
6. Is the ground colour "wet", or painted in scales?
7. Do the grounds contain vase- or mirror-shaped panels surrounded by Rococo gilt frames?
8. Are the marks right?

Worcester (1751–74)

The Worcester factory was founded on 4 June 1751, by a group of 15 gentlemen, merchants, and craftsmen, including Dr John Wall, who managed it until 1774. In 1752, the factory bought out Benjamin Lund's Bristol factory. By combining Dr Wall's soft-paste formula with Bristol's experience and technical expertise, Worcester was soon manufacturing a surprisingly sophisticated range of products.

Soft-paste

Early Worcester porcelain contained soapstone, which enable it to withstand boiling water. This made it particularly suitable for the tea and coffee wares that the factory produced in large quantities.

• The body has a greenish tinge, which can be easily seen when the piece is

A Worcester coffee cup, painted with the "Warbler" pattern. c.1758 2.5in (6.5cm) high G

This mark c.1755–75

held up to the light, and there are tiny, peppery pinpricks.

• The greenish or bluish glaze is close-fitting and free from crackle.

Artefacts

Worcester produced many artefacts that were not imported from China. They added Chinese-style decoration to shapes that were copied from fashionable silver of the time. These included sauceboats, cream jugs, pickle dishes, saltcellars, and inkwells – mainly in the Rococo taste.

Moulding

Worcester wares were thinly potted. Most large pieces tended to warp or sag. The moulded surface helped to disguise flaws in the glaze. The most famous example of

A transfer-printed mug, decorated with William Pitt, the Elder. c.1760 3.25in (8cm) high E

A pair of Worcester scale-blue Kakiemon vases and covers. c.1770 11.75in (30cm) high D

more than 6in (15cm) high

• the overall shape is derived from silverware
  • the ear-shaped handle with a high scrolled thumbpiece looks a bit like a script "3"
    • the tentative chinoiserie decorations are painted in a bold hybrid palette drawn from both *famille verte* and *famille rose*
  • the inside of the rim is decorated with small ribboned objects
  • the moulding is enhanced by the bright sparkle of the glaze.

Sauceboats are among the most common early Worcester products. Most, like this example (see opposite above), are decorated in a monochrome underglaze blue, which

this moulding is the cabbage leaf pattern used on the jug shown on p.136.

"Pegging"

All Worcester products have a narrow, unglazed margin round the interior of the footrim. This was caused by a process known as "pegging", which was designed to prevent excess glaze from spilling over onto the kiln. Before the firing began, the excess glaze was scraped away from the inner footrim with a wooden peg.

Wares

This moulded hexagonal cream jug has many features typical of early Worcester:

• it is quite small – few early wares are

A Worcester "Chelsea Ewer" cream jug, painted in the London atelier of James Giles. c.1772 3.5in (9cm) high F

A Worcester chinoiserie sauceboat. c.1775
7in (18cm) long G

can vary from a soft, greyish blue to a
deep, almost black cobalt.

Scale blue

One Worcester speciality that is
currently undervalued is scale blue,
also known as blue scale, as on these
Kakiemon vases and covers (see
opposite above). The wares have a unique
background created with tiny painted
scales to break up the solid effect of the
dark blue. The reserved panels were
painted in vivid colours with "fancy",
exotic birds and out-of-scale insects.

Transfer printing

In around 1756 Josiah Holdship
perfected a method where a pattern
engraved into a metal printing plate
could be transferred onto unglazed
porcelain. Instead of relying on
individual painters, finely detailed
patterns could be printed in underglaze
blue in quantity. Worcester used
transfer printing extensively in the
1760s and 1770s but Holdship's

technique was never patented and other
factories soon copied Worcester's lead.

Marks

From the 1760s onwards, Worcester
marked its wares with a crescent in
underglaze blue. This was copied
at Lowestoft and should also not be
confused with the "C" of Caughley.

Worcester blue
crescent mark
c.1755–90

A Worcester leaf-moulded cream jug. c.1765
3.5in (9cm) high F

This mark c.1770–7

Flight and Flight & Barr

A Worcester dish, in Sèvres style, decorated with exotic birds. c.1775 10in (25.5cm) wide D

1. Is the porcelain hard-paste?
2. If the piece is part of a dinner or dessert service, is the porcelain hard, white, and translucent, with a glassy glaze?
3. Is the gilding of unusually high quality?
4. Is the decoration of the panels extremely detailed and exact?
5. If the piece is a plaque, does it have an extravagant gilt frame?
6. If a Rococo plate, does the piece have only six bracket lobes on the rim?
7. If a vessel, does it have angular handles and loop knops on its cover?
8. If a cup, is it a severe bucket-shape?

A Flight and Barr Worcester vase and cover, painted with a view of Hampton Court country house. c.1795 14.5in (37cm) high B

Worcester (1783–c.1807)

After Dr Wall retired, in 1774, his factory was managed by another partner, William Davis, until it was bought by its London agent, Thomas Flight, in 1783. Three years later his chief decorator, Robert Chamberlain, left to form a rival firm, first decorating porcelain from Caughley and then producing his own hybrid hard-paste. Within a decade there were two thriving Worcester firms.

Meanwhile, the original firm was going through several changes of name. It was after Flight's death, in 1792, that his two sons went into partnership with Martin Barr and began to trade as Flight & Barr, and in 1807, when they were joined by another Barr, their firm's name became Barr, Flight & Barr. During these years, the first factory's wares were unsurpassed. A number of the leading English decorators worked there and most unusually, they were paid by the hour and not by the piece.

Paste and glaze

Under Thomas Flight's management, the soft-paste became a more brilliant hard-paste, the glaze became more refined, and the potting became more even and a little thicker. However, both glaze and body maintained their overall greyish appearance.

A Barr, Flight & Barr Worcester stand. c.1800 5.5in (14cm) wide G

This mark Barr, Flight & Barr c.1807–13

141

Flight, Barr & Barr 1813–40

A pair of Worcester Flight, Barr & Barr vases, with continuous landscapes. c.1820
6.5in (16.5cm) high D

1. Does the decoration cover the entire piece?
2. Is the painted decoration of almost photographic quality?
3. Does the piece have "Greek-key" borders?
4. Is the gilding of superb quality?
5. Does the piece show Rococo influence?
6. Does the piece have Neo-classical features?
7. Is it in the Sèvres style?
8. Is it fully marked (see opposite)?

Worcester (1813–40)

When Martin Barr died in 1813 the firm changed its name again, this time to Flight, Barr & Barr. The styles continued and the quality improved, but the rival factory of Chamberlain's was flourishing.

In 1840 Chamberlain took over Flight, Barr & Barr, and in 1852 Chamberlain's was itself bought out by the partnership of Kerr and Binns. Meanwhile, a third factory had been established in Worcester. In 1800 Thomas Grainger, a relation of Chamberlain, established a firm that became known as Grainger, Lee and Co., which continued trading until the end of the 19thC imitating Chamberlain's products and reproducing Wall's early wares.

A Flight Barr & Barr Worcester campana vase. c1820 6.75in (17cm) high E

Neo-classicism

In the early part of the 19thC, Neo-classicism remained the dominant theme at the factory run by the Barr and Flight families, but the decorations became progressively less restrained. Tablewares were produced and, to a lesser extent, mantelshelf pieces. Rococo-shaped plates, which reflect the Sèvres style of the 1760s, have much in common with plates from other British factories, but with subtle differences:

• The kidney-shaped dish has a more complex wavy rim than the equivalent dish from Coalport or Spode.
• The essentially Rococo decoration also includes Neo-classical features, such as festoons and swags.

A Flight, Barr & Barr Worcester ceremonial tureen cover and liner. c.1820 32in (12.5cm) wide D

This mark c.1813-40

Royal Worcester

*A Royal Worcester vase and cover,
painted with swans by Charles
Baldwyn. 1900 17in (43cm) high C*

1. Is the overall decoration of a very high standard?
2. Does it cover the object?
3. Is the gilding of exceptional quality?
4. Is the painting of Highland cattle, swans, fruit, or sheep?
5. Is the piece signed by Charles Baldwyn, Harry Davis, James
   Stinton, Harry Stinton, or John Stinton?
6. Is the piece marked (see opposite)?

Royal Worcester (1862–present)

While concentrating on tea and dinner wares, Royal Worcester is particularly known for individually decorated vases and pot-pourris in Classical shapes. Royal Worcester understood Japanese taste better than any other English factory, including Minton, and produced many "Japonaise" wares. Also introduced were double-walled vases, teapots, and decorative items that were produced by George Owen.

Royal Worcester kept pace with public demand for novelty in design with the development of a wide range of new materials and glazes, including glazed and underglazed Parian earthenware, majolica, and bone china. The firm concentrated on the production of figures and vases.

A Royal Worcester vase and cover, painted with ducks, by James Stinton. 1908 16.5in (42cm) high D

A Royal Worcester pot-pourri vase and cover, painted with highland cattle, by John Stinton. 1921 13in (33cm) high D

Royal Worcester miniatures are popular and less common than Royal Crown Derby, although arguably of inferior quality.

At the beginning of the 20thC Royal Worcester allowed the painters to sign their work. China patterns were named from the 1920s onwards.

From 1891 "Royal Worcester England" was added round the standard mark. From 1892 a dot was added every year.

A Royal Worcester vase, painted by Harry Davis, shape 1969. 1912 16in (40.5cm) high D

Caughley

A Caughley small cylindrical mug, printed with the "Parrot Pecking Fruit" pattern. c.1780 3.25in (8cm) high F

1. Does the paste have an orange glow in transmitted light?
2. Is the piece transfer-printed?
3. Does it emulate Chinese porcelain?
4. From c.1780 is there French influence on the style and design?
5. Is the piece gilded?
6. Is it decorated with the "Willow" pattern?

A Caughley caddy spoon, printed with pagoda boats. c.1780 4in (10cm) high G

A Caughley dessert dish, made for the Marquis of Donegal. c.1793 10.25in (26cm) wide G

Caughley (c.1775–99)

In the early to mid-1770s, Thomas Turner, who had possibly trained as an engraver at the Worcester Porcelain Company, came from Worcester to the Caughley works, or "Salopian China Manufactory", which was adapted to cater for his knowledge of soft-paste porcelain. This required the shipment of soapstone and china clays from Devon and Cornwall.

From the very beginning, Caughley specialized in transfer-printed wares, blue and white ware that emulated imported Chinese porcelain, and also for which it became famous. In 1775 Robert Hancock, the pre-eminent and pioneer engraver at Worcester, joined Turner at Caughley.

The Caughley moulded, cabbage-leaf jugs with mask-head spout (which were originally known as "Dutch jugs") are perhaps the best-known articles made by the firm. Examples decorated in underglaze blue normally bear the "S" or "C" initial marks.

The Coalport partners took over the Caughley works in October 1799.

A cabbage-leaf mask-head spout jug, printed with the "Fisherman and Cormorant" pattern. c.1790 8.5in (21.5cm) high H

This mark 1775–99

Lowestoft

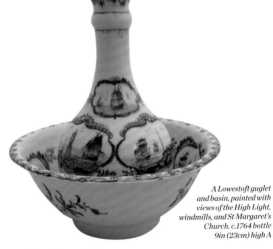

A Lowestoft guglet and basin, painted with views of the High Light, windmills, and St Margaret's Church. c.1764 bottle 9in (23cm) high A

1. Is the porcelain soft-paste?
2. Is there any brownish discoloration?
3. If the piece is decorated in underglaze blue, is the blue slightly blurred and greyish?
4. Is the glaze greenish or greyish, and has it pooled to a more intense colour in crevices?
5. If the piece is a coffee cup or pot, does the handle have a kick-back terminal on the lower joint?
6. If the piece is a cup, does it have a conical base and a wedge-shaped footrim?

Lowestoft (1757–c.1800)

The Lowestoft factory was founded in 1757 by Robert Browne and three partners. Situated in a remote fishing port on the coast of Suffolk, it was a long way from the fashionable marketplaces and it was completely out of touch with changing tastes, but it survived for almost 50 years at a time when Chelsea, Bow, Derby, and Worcester were at their peak. Lowestoft is a phosphatic porcelain, similar to Bow, with a tendency to discoloration. The glaze is not particularly glassy and has a slightly greenish or greyish tone, which pools to a more intense colour in crevices. All the wares made during the factory's first ten years are decorated in a cold underglaze blue, which varies from a greyish to an almost black tone. The influence of Worcester is often obvious, not only in the chinoiserie designs but also in the moulded

A Lowestoft "A Trifle from Lowestoft" inkwell. c.1800 2.75in (7cm) diam D

decorations, but the actual shapes of the wares were usually derived from salt-glaze stoneware. From the mid-1760s overglaze colours and underglaze blue printing were introduced. The factory also made a number of figures: cats, sheep, pugdogs, and putti. Some Lowestoft wares have the Worcester crescent. Most underglaze blue and some coloured wares pre-1770s have numerals on the inside of the footrim.

A miniature Lowestoft blue and white teapot and cover, painted with sailing boats. c.1760–70 3in (7.5cm) high F

A Lowestoft brown and white pug dog. c1790 D

Liverpool

*A Chaffers Liverpool vase
and cover. c.1755–60
12in (30.5cm) high D*

1. Has the paste discoloured?
2. Is the glaze bluish or greenish?
3. Are there areas of peppering?
4. Is the decoration blue and white chinoiserie?
5. Is the cobalt inky black?
6. Is the appearance like a greyish early Worcester?
7. Are there tiny areas of iridescence?
8. If the piece is a bowl, is the footrim undercut?
9. If the piece is a teapot or coffee can, is the footrim wedge-shaped?
10. Does the painting look a bit clumsy?
11. If the decoration is printed, does it look primitive?

The Liverpool factories

There were several small porcelain factories in Liverpool in the second half of the 18thC, but there are so few records that it is sometimes difficult to attribute pieces to specific factories. However, it is known that most of the factories used a soapstone porcelain, like that used at Worcester and Caughley. The greyish appearance of most Liverpool porcelain is in fact very similar to Worcester's, but it tends to suffer from peppering and the potting is variable. Figures are rare. The most popular products are blue and white tea and coffee services. But decorators also used enamels, either

A Gilbody figure of a Levantine lady. c.1754–60 7in (18cm) high E

in a style similar to Worcester's, or in a harsh *famille rose* palette, which can be confused with New Hall or even Lowestoft.

The main factories were:
Richard Chaffer (1754–65),
Philip Christian (1765–76),
Samuel Gilbody (c.1754–61)
William Reid and others (c.1755–70),
John and Jane Pennington (c.1770–94),
and Seth Pennington and John Part (1778–1803).

A Chaffers Liverpool coffee pot and cover, painted with the "Jumping Boy" pattern. c.1758 7.75in (19.5cm) high D

A Samuel Gilbody coffee cup. c.1755–60 3in (7.5cm) high E

Liverpool porcelain is characterized by vertical footrims or undercut on the inner surface; flat bases to mugs; areas of blue ground marbled in gold; and a blued glaze giving a "thundercloud" effect where thick under the base. With so many factories in close proximity in Liverpool, it is certain that workers moved from one to another. It is important to study the subtle variations of the glaze, body, and colour of the blue and white as many factories copied the shapes and designs that were fashionable at the time. In general,

A rare Philip Christian Liverpool cream jug. c.1770 3.75in (9.5cm) high F

looking at the quality of the underglaze blue: Chaffers and Christian's is light and bright, Gilbody's is often blurred. The factories of Philip Christian and Seth Pennington were roughly a quarter of the size of Worcester. By comparison, the short-lived factories of Samuel Gilbody and William Reid were tiny – perhaps only a twentieth of Worcester's size. Examples from the small factories are rare and hard to find. It is worth searching them out as they can sometimes be very valuable.

Richard Chaffers & Co.

Richard Chaffers made soapstone-type porcelain featuring mainly Oriental designs at Shaw's Brow until 1765. Many wares were enamelled with a Chinese scene in polychrome. Philip Christian & Co. took over the factory when Richard Chaffers died and produced similar designs until 1778.

• The blue and white Chaffers coffee

A Philip Christian & Co. Liverpool vase. c.1770 9.75in (25cm) high E

pot and vase and cover (see pp.150–1) have a greyish blue body and the dark cobalt blue is typical of most Liverpool factories.

• All have a bluish glaze that has gathered in very dark pools on the inside of their footrims.

Chaffers wares are usually very translucent and almost white, and they appear slightly green when held up to a strong light. The phosphate in the porcelain formula has caused discoloration in areas where the glaze is thin.

Samuel Gilbody

Next door to Chaffers, Samuel Gilbody took over his father's earthenware

A William Reid chinoiserie teapot and cover.
c.1755–60 6.75in (17cm) high G

business and switched to the production of enamelled porcelain at his China Manufactory from about 1755 until his bankruptcy in 1760.

The Gilbody figure of a Levantine lady (see p.151), made in the late 1760s, is extremely rare. Similar figures were made at Longton Hall, Bow and Chelsea.

Philip Christian

Philip Christian continued to run Chaffers factory with his widow after Chaffers died in 1765.

This early Christian's cream jug (see opposite above) has the slightly bluish glaze typical of Liverpool porcelain, especially where it has gathered near the foot rim.

• The piece is made out of a chalky, plaster-like paste which was typical of Christian's factory.

A William Reid Liverpool tea bowl and saucer.
c.1758 G

An early Pennington's Liverpool creamer.
c.1780 5in (12.5cm) long G

• The delicately painted enamels are not unlike those used at Worcester in the 1750s.

There is some peppering around the base.

William Reid

On 12 November 1756 William Reid's first advert for porcelain produced in Liverpool appeared in the *Liverpool Advertiser*. He used an underglaze blue and Oriental designs on an almost opaque body. The company went bankrupt, however, in June 1761 but the business continued under William Ball. It was finally sold in July 1763 to Thomas Lewis.

The Penningtons

Seth Pennington and John Part

This partnership took over Christian's factory from 1778 and continued to make porcelain on the site, producing wares in a similar style to the previous owners probably having bought the moulds. Their porcelain was of the bone-ash type. Seth Pennington produced popular Worcester and Caughley patterns, such as the "Fisherman" and "Pleasure Boat".

James Pennington & Co.

James was one of Seth's older brothers and had been in partnership with Richard Chaffers. He took over the factory once owned by William Reid c.1762. He possibly made a soapstone porcelain there. He moved to Park Lane Pothouse in 1767 changing to bone-ash porcelain until at least 1773.

A John and Jane Pennington Liverpool teapot and cover. c.1770–94 7in (18cm) high H

John and Jane Pennington

John Pennington and his wife Jane also had two porcelain factories: Copperas Hill, c.1770–79 and Folly Lane, 1779–86 which were continued by his widow Jane until 1794. In 1779 they announced in a Liverpool newspaper that they were making "Elegant, cheap and serviceable china ware, which are, for brilliancy of colour, equal to any made in Great Britain".

A rare Pennington's Liverpool spoon tray. c.1785 6.25in (16cm) high G

A Pennington's Liverpool jug. c.1780 4.25in (11cm) high G

The pieces shown have the general greyish look of Liverpool porcelain. The early Pennington's creamer shown (opposite above) is slightly warmer.

Creamers

Cream was served in vessels that resemble sauceboats but are smaller. As a shape they are unique to Britain. Pennington's made creamers, or cream ewers as they are sometimes called, until c.1790 when the fashion seemingly died out.

Marks

There are no factory marks for the Liverpool concerns.

Wares are unmarked except for a few spurious Worcester crescents.

Plymouth & Champion's Bristol

*A Plymouth mug, painted
with exotic birds. c.1770
5.25in (13cm) high E*

1. Is the porcelain hard-paste and greyish?
2. Are figures press-moulded?
3. Is the glaze yellowish?
4. Are there dark, smoky patches?
5. If the pieces is a ware, is it a Rococo shape with Neo-classical decorations?
6. Do small hollowwares have elaborately moulded cartouches?
7. If the piece is a figure, is it heavy and does it look as though it has sagged or split in places?

A Plymouth sauceboat, of moulded Rococo form. c.1768–70 5.5in (14cm) wide E

A Plymouth mug, painted with colourful birds. c.1768–70 6in (15.5cm) high E

Plymouth (1768–70)

Established in 1768 by a chemist, William Cookworthy, Plymouth and Cookworthy's Bristol were the first English factories to make true hard-paste porcelain. He discovered the essential china clay and china stone and obtained a patent giving him the sole right to produce hard-paste porcelain until 1782. Plymouth produced the usual range of wares, decorated in either underglaze blue or polychrome

A Plymouth coffee pot and cover, painted with the "Mansfield" pattern. c.1770 9.25in (23.5cm) high E

enamels, and a range of naïve, massively modelled figures with splits in their sides. Almost every product had a flaw, and so in 1770 Cookworthy moved his factory to the important ceramics centre of Bristol.

Cookworthy's Bristol (1770–74).

• The moulded cartouches are among the most elaborate in English porcelain.
• Unusually, the glaze does not suffer from darkening, although it has a characteristic yellowness.

A Plymouth sauceboat, painted with Chinese river landscapes. c.1770 8.5in (21.5cm) long E

157

A Champion's Bristol cup and saucer, from the "Butts" service. c.1775 F

Champion's Bristol (1774–81)

In 1774 Cookworthy assigned his factory to a young Quaker, Richard Champion, who introduced designs and shapes in the Neo-classical taste. However, the factory never knew financial stability and closed in 1781. The patent passed to New Hall (see pp.160–1).

*A Champion's Bristol sugar bowl. c.1775
4.5in (11.5cm) wide G*

Paste and glaze

Both factories used a greyish white paste with a cold, glassy, yellowish glaze. On larger pieces it tended to sag or split in the kiln, but at Bristol there was less darkening caused by misfiring.

Neo-classical decoration was the most popular form on these early Champion's Bristol tearwares, made around 1775. The gilding on Champion's wares from this period is of a very high quality. The ear-shaped handle with a "wishbone" projection at the bottom (see opposite below right) was used on many Bristol cups, teapots, and larger vessels in the mid-1770s.

Champion's Bristol figures are relatively large. The rockwork bases on the figures were usually washed in a vibrant green and edged in yellow and russet. Earlier Plymouth figures tend to have Rococo bases.

Chinese porcelain was still available at modest prices and the wares produced at Plymouth and then at Bristol were rarely competitive.

Fakes

Plymouth bell-shaped tankards, such as the one on p.156, became so popular in the 19thC that a number of fakes were produced both in England and in

France. These fakes usually carry the Plymouth mark, but the paste has no greyish tone, the palette is completely different, and the attempt to recreate the bird patterns of Plymouth's great decorator Michel Soqui is much too loose and lacks detail.

Marks

The mark used only at Plymouth was a combination of 2 and 4, the alchemical sign for tin, which was the main product of Cornwall before Cookworthy found the china clay that was soon to be used by every English factory.

The Bristol mark is a simple cross in overglaze blue, sometimes accompanied by a "B", or else the crossed swords of Meissen in underglaze blue.

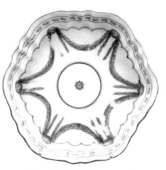

A Champion's Bristol teapot stand, typically decorated with swags. c.1775 5.25in (13cm) diam H

A Champion's Bristol cup. c.1775 2.5in (6.5cm) high H

A Champion's Bristol chocolate cup with basketweave moulding. 1773-76 4.75in (12cm) high G

New Hall

A New Hall "Birds in Landscape" saucer dish, painted by Fidèle Duvivier. c.1790
8in (20.5cm) diam G

1. Is the glaze thick, dull, and greenish?
2. Are there any pools in the glaze and are they filled with small bubbles?
3. Are the wares fluted or moulded?
4. Are the shapes similar to those used by Worcester or Caughley?
5. Is puce prominent in the palette?
6. Is the piece decorated in the manner of late Chinese export ware?

A New Hall cup and saucer, "Basket of Flowers" pattern, pattern no. 171. c.1785–90 5in (12.5cm) diam H

A New Hall teapot and cover, decorated in the Chinese Export style, pattern no. 273. c.1790 H

New Hall (1781–c.1830)

The second Staffordshire porcelain factory (Longton Hall was the first) was founded by a group of local potters who bought Richard Champion's patent for hybrid hard-paste in 1781. After operating briefly and unsuccessfully at Tunstall, they moved to nearby Shelton in 1782, and it was this second factory that became known as New Hall.

Paste and glaze

As it is made to the same formula, the greyish New Hall paste is inevitably very similar to Champion's Bristol paste, and the wares suffer from many of the same weaknesses, such as wreathing. The glaze, on the other hand, is completely different. Thick, dull, and greenish, it sometimes leaves areas uncovered, and it tends to gather in pools that are filled with small bubbles.

Wares

The New Hall factory made no figures and very few decorative wares. The majority of its products are teawares, and apart from these it seems to have made mostly dessert wares, jugs, and punch bowls.

Shapes and decoration

In the early phase of production, up until about 1800, most wares were fluted or moulded in shapes very similar to those used at Worcester and Caughley. However, despite the Neoclassical shapes, the decorations

A New Hall helmet-shaped chinoiserie milk jug. c.1785 3.75in (9.5cm) high H

A New Hall sucrier. c.1805
7.25in (18.5cm) wide G

in on-glaze gold. This sucrier (see left) is a good example of the Classical shape with the scene on the side applied using Warburton's patent, but, as with most examples of this technique, the gold has faded over the years and lost its crispness, and now has a brownish tinge. The knop modelled in the form of a Chinese hat is particularly characteristic of New Hall.

often followed the designs of late Chinese export ware, particularly *famille rose* flower patterns and figure subjects, which were usually printed and then colour washed. The finest and rarest of the early wares, such as those on p.160, were decorated by the French artist Fidèle Duvivier, who was known particularly for his landscapes and exotic birds in landscapes. Later wares followed the Neo-classical shapes and designs used by many other factories, but there was also one decorative technique that was unique to New Hall. Known as Warburton's patent after one of the founding partners, it was used for painting scenes

A New Hall "Imari" sugar bowl and cover,
pattern no. 446. c.1800–10
5.25in (13cm) wide H

This teapot is typical of the first phase of production at the New Hall factory. The basic silver shape was copied by several other factories, but the edges detailed in enamel (usually puce or blue), the flowers with dotted heads, and the fan-like motifs in the frieze are characteristic New Hall decorations.

Some of these early teapots have little feet shaped like rosettes.

This teapot (see below), which was made soon after 1810, represents the second and much more sophisticated phase of production at New Hall. Many factories used this high-galleried, Neo-classical silver shape; and the underglaze blue panels at either end, delicately painted in gilt with palmettes and fern-like vegetation, were a very popular form of decoration.

A New Hall coffee can, pattern no. 1153. c.1812–15 2.25in (6cm) high H

One of the most popular decorations was many adaptations of the Imari palette as shown on the sugar bowl (see opposite below), and coffee can (see above). These brightly coloured wares were particularly in fashion from 1800 to 1815. In c.1812 the New Hall factory converted from hard-paste to bone china.

Marks

A few bone china wares bear the printed mark "New Hall" surrounded by two circles. Earlier wares have no mark, but the large pieces are marked with the letter "N" followed by a pattern number below 1940, usually in red.

An early 19thC New Hall chinoiserie teapot, cover, and stand. G

Davenport

*A Davenport
porcelain plate,
painted with roses,
hollyhocks, phlox, and
Morning Glory. c.1820
9.25in (23.5cm) diam F*

1. Is the decoration of a very superior quality?
2. Is the flower painting of high quality?
3. Is the flower painting by James Holland?
4. Has the painting an Oriental, either Chinese or Imari, influence?
5. Is the piece reminiscent of Derby porcelain?
6. Are the colours muted?
7. Is the ground colour a deep blue or green?

An early 19thC Davenport porcelain vase, painted in the "Chinese Temple" pattern. 6.25in (16cm) high H

A Davenport porcelain bough pot and cover. c.1815 7.75in (19.5cm) wide F

Davenport (c.1793–1887)

Another very important Staffordshire factory was the one run by John Davenport at Longport. Originally an earthenware pottery, the factory began to make hard-paste bulb pots and bone china wares c.1800, and from about 1812 onwards it then began to concentrate on bone china tea as well as dessert services.

At the beginning of the 19thC the factory was very fashionable and numbered the Prince Regent among its customers.

With its deep blue and green ground colours along with floral designs,

Davenport decoration is of a very high standard. The painters in Davenport would often imitate Derby, but they also developed designs of their own, which include Imari patterns, having been influenced by Oriental works.

A Davenport "Etruscan Shape" teacup, coffee cup, and saucer. c.1820–5 H

Coalport

A pair of Coalport ice pails, covers, and liners, richly decorated with orange and blue gilded bands.
c.1810 11in (28cm) high E

1. Is the piece a greyish hybrid hard-paste (pre-1820)?
2. Is the glaze dull and grainy?
3. Is the piece made of fine white bone china (post-1820)?
4. Is it liberally encrusted with flowers?
5. If a plate, does the rim have six lobes with shallow notches?
6. Is the piece decorated in a bright Imari palette?
7. Does it have a fractional pattern number?

Coalport (1790–present)

The Coalport factory in Shropshire was founded in the 1790s by John Rose. Rose had trained at the Caughley porcelain manufactory in Shropshire. He bought the Caughley manufactory in 1799, the Nantgarw porcelain manufactory in 1819, and the Swansea porcelain manufactory, with their repertory of moulds. He employed William Billingsley, formerly at Nantgarw, as chief painter, and Billingsley's chemist, Walker, who initiated at Coalport a maroon glaze and brought the Nantgarw technical recipes to Rose at Coalport.

In 1820 Rose received the gold medal of the Society of Arts for his feldspar porcelain and an improved, lead-free glaze, with which the enamel colours fused in firing. Favourite patterns were

A Coalport coffee can, painted with an artist's palette and brushes. c.1800 3.5in (9cm) high G

the "Worm Sprig" and the "Tournai Sprig" introduced by Billingsley at Pinxton, the Dresden-inspired "Berlin China Edge", and the blue transfer "Willow" pattern and "Blue dragon" pattern. During the 1830s the factory initiated the practice of applying a light transfer-printed

A Caughley/Coalport spoon tray, painted with the "Tower" pattern. c.1798 6in (15.5cm) wide F

A Coalport plate, painted with a flower spray. c.1810 8.5in (21.5cm) diam H

A pair of Coalport vases, painted with birds among trees and flowers. c.1860 12in (30.5cm) high E

blue outline, to guide the painters. This preserved some of the freedom of hand-painted decoration, while it enabled Rose to keep up the pace of production. The technique was widely adopted by other manufactories during the 19thC. When John Rose died in 1841, the enterprise was continued under the former name "John Rose & Co." by his nephew W. F. Rose and William Pugh. Now housed at Stoke-on-Trent, the factory is still in production.

Paste and glaze
Until 1820 the factory made a greyish hard-paste, and covered it with a dull grainy glaze.

Wares
Coalport concentrated on table, and decorative wares.

• In the 1870s the factory began to make the flower-encrusted Rococo pieces for which it was to become famous, and after the Great Exhibition in 1851 it produced a large number of Sèvres-style vases with *bleu celeste* or *rose Pompadour* grounds.

Decoration
The most prominent among the many decorative themes are:
• Neo-classical designs with emphasis on a drab or restricted palette
• Imari patterns
• delicate bouquets of summer flowers dominated by pink
• landscape views; rarely named.

Ground colours
The most popular ground colours on services are:

A pair of Coalport vases and covers, painted by John Randall. c.1870 13.5in (34cm) high G

- apple green
- dark blue
- beige.

Marks

Early Coalport pieces were not marked, but some later wares were marked with a script "Coalport"; and many of the Rococo and flower-encrusted vases were marked "Coalbrookdale".

Pattern numbers were used in marks after c.1820.

These pieces, made between 1800 and 1805, are composed of a greyish, hybrid hard-paste. The Imari pattern and the knop are unique to Coalport, while the acanthus-scroll handles and the six-lobed plate are typical.

The ice pails in the main picture (see p.166), was made at Coalport early in the

19thC. The decoration was set against a solid dark blue ground that was more characteristic of the early stages of the factory. However, the shape is very typical of Coalport, and so too are the entwined stalk knop and the flaring Sèvres-type foliage handles.

A Coalport vase and cover, painted with a castle in a landscape. c.1900 10in (25.5cm) high G

Minton

A Minton decorated pâte-sur-pâte
*vase, by Louis Solon. 1889
20.5in (52cm) high A*

1. If the piece is soft-paste, is it thinly potted with a greyish glaze?
2. If the piece is hard-paste, is it flawless and is the glaze very smooth?
3. Is the decoration on the soft-paste Neo-classical?
4. Is the decoration on the hard-paste Neo-classical?
5. Does the piece show evidence of Rococo Revival'?
6. Is there excessive use of gilding?
7. Has the *pâte-sur-pâte* technique been used?
8. Does the piece have a pattern number and a date cipher?

Minton (1793–present)

Minton was founded in 1793 by Thomas Minton. The factory has always maintained a consistently high quality and has been one of the most innovative in Britain.

Paste and glaze

The early soft-paste, from 1798 to c.1810, is thinly potted with a slightly greyish glaze and sometimes has fine black specks in it, especially on the base. The later hard-paste, after 1821, is among the finest and cleanest of all British porcelains. It is rarely flawed, and the glaze is thin and extremely smooth, particularly compared to the more musliny glaze on the soft-paste.

Wares

Early soft-paste wares were painted or printed with Neo-classical designs. Later hard-paste wares were usually copied from 18thC Sèvres or Meissen, with moulded borders and pierced rims. The centre is painted in a sentimental style that is typical of several other contemporary factories, but few could match the quality of the basketweave.

Decorative wares

Minton's decorative wares included flower-encrusted objects similar to those made at Coalbrookdale and Rockingham. The factory also made Sèvres-style vases and jars with coloured grounds.

In 1870 the modeller Marc-Louis Solon

arrived from Sèvres and introduced the *pâte-sur-pâte* technique, whereby white slip was built up and carved on a dark coloured ground, such as pink, green, or blue. The painstaking process often took several weeks to complete and was extremely costly, but the effect could be stunning.

The *pâte-sur-pâte* technique was continued well into the 20thC, but, although the quality was still very high, the pieces lacked the vitality of the 19thC examples.

Marks

The earliest mark was based on the interlaced "L"s of Sèvres.

The mid-19thC mark was an impressed "Minton", and after 1863 "Mintons". Until c.1900 alchemical-style date ciphers were also impressed. Pattern numbers were also used.

Minton figures

A pair of Minton "The Grand Turk" and "Turkish Lady" porcelain figures. c.1825–35 5in (12.5cm) high G

1. If a figure, is it heavy for its size?
2. If the piece is a figure, is it very elaborately decorated and more highly coloured than other English figures?
3. Does the figure represent romantic rural life?
4. Is the base of the figure heavily modelled with stiff Rococo scrolls (see opposite)?
5. Is the figure made of Parian?

Minton figures

The early Minton figures were mostly romantic shepherds and shepherdesses in 18thC costume. These were either elaborately decorated with flowered clothes or else left in the biscuit.

• Other subjects included foreign costumes and famous characters, such as theatrical personalities.

• In the 1830s Minton began producing figures in an unglazed bone china body, called "bisque".

• In the late 1840s Minton began to model figures in Parian, a type of porcelain that looks like marble.

A Minton bone china floral group. c1835. 7in (18cm) high G

• Most of the Parian figures are portrait busts or statuettes romantic maidens. As well as figures, Minton made a large number of candlestick groups. The heavily modelled Rococo scrolls on the base are typical of the figures as well as the candlesticks.

The detailed features and the dense flowers on the costumes are characteristic of Minton. Faces are usually highly coloured. Although Derby and other factories made similar figures, their decoration is usually a more simplistic style.

A pair of Minton porcelain figural candlesticks. c.1835. 9in (23cm) high G

Spode

A pair of Spode porcelain violet baskets and pierced covers, pattern no. 1139. c.1815 E

1. Is the piece made of bone china?
2. Is the bone china pure white in appearance?
3. Is the piece very thinly potted?
4. If the piece is part of a service, is it moulded in relief?
5. Is the decoration an Imari pattern?
6. Is the ground colour lavender blue?
7. Is the gilding of a high quality?
8. Is the piece marked with a pattern number in red?

Spode (1776–present)

The Spode factory at Stoke-on-Trent in Staffordshire was founded by Josiah Spode in 1776. By 1800 it had developed probably the first formula for English bone china. In 1813 the founder's son, Josiah II, went into partnership with W. T. Copeland, and in 1833 he was bought out by Copeland and T. Garrett. The factory is still in operation and is now merged with Worcester.

Paste and glaze

The paste is pure white, close-grained, and as smooth as icing (confectioner's) sugar. The glaze is thin, very smooth, and white.

Wares

The majority of Spode porcelain were

An early 19thC Spode Imari ice pail, cover, and liner, pattern no. 1599. 12.25in (31cm) high F

tablewares and ornamental wares, which until about 1850 were almost all derived from Roman or Etruscan forms.

Decoration

The factory used various printing techniques, and in the early years it specialized in bat printing – using bats of soft glue instead of paper transfers to produce monochrome vignettes of landscapes and Neo-classical scenes.

• Decorative wares were more ambitiously painted with densely packed botanical subjects, topographical views, and copies of Old Master paintings.

• Like Derby, Spode produced a wide range of Imari patterns, but the Spode versions were much more meticulously painted.

A Spode perfume bottle. c.1805–10 4in (10cm) wide E

Copeland Spode

*A pair of Copeland
Neo-classical
porcelain ewers. c.1875
14.5in (37cm) high E*

1. Is the decoration/painting of high quality?
2. Does it have a jewelled ground?
3. Are wares covered in high-quality gilding?
4. Does it have a strong ground colour – often green, blue, or
   bright pink?
5. If a figure or bust is it Parian?
6. Does it have impressed date marks showing the month letter and
   the last two numerals of the year?

A Copeland Spode cabinet cup, cover, and stand.
c.1835. 5in (12.5cm) high H

A pair of Copeland porcelain pedestal jars.
c.1875 18.5in (47cm) high E

Copeland Spode (1847-present)

The Spode-Copeland factory was the first to develop Parian, a form of porcelain simulating marble. From 1844 onwards it produced a wide range of Parian figures and busts after the leading sculptors of the day. Almost every piece was marked with the sculptor's name.

Spode produced a considerable number of tall, bucket-shaped spill vases, which were plain, or decorated with the typical borders of applied beads. Typical features of the fine wares made by Spode in the first quarter of the 19thC:

A Copeland Parian bust, the
"Veiled Bride", after Raphael
Monti. 1860s
11in (28cm) high F

• delicate raised white patterns on the borders of the piece
• butterfly handles on the sauce tureens
• precise, large-scale botanical painting.
Spode's portrait busts of statesmen and large-scale models of scantily clad maidens were among the most popular Parian subjects.

Marks

Before 1830 the most common mark was a hand-painted "SPODE". By 1820 the mark was also being printed.

After 1833 "COPELAND & GARRETT" was written in a circle with "LATE SPODE" in the middle of the mark. Pattern numbers are usually be painted in red.

Nantgarw and Swansea

A Welsh porcelain campana vase, painted by William Billingsley, marked "NANTGARW". c.1813–23 10.75in (27.5cm) high A

1. Is the paste pure white?
2. Is the glaze smooth and glassy and virtually flawless?
3. Is the piece either pure white or duck-egg blue by transmitted light?
4. Are there three spurs arranged in a triangle of small iridescent circles on the base?
5. If the piece is a plate, is the border moulded in shallow relief with Rococo cartouches?
6. Is the flower decoration of a very high quality?

Nantgarw and Swansea (1813–26)

Probably the finest porcelain made in Britain in the early 19thC came from South Wales.

Hoping to rival the quality of French porcelain, the great Derby decorator William Billingsley set up a factory at Nantgarw in 1813 with financial support from William Weston Young. Their porcelain was the most difficult of all to fire. Up to 90 per cent of it was lost in the kiln.

After only a year they moved to Swansea to join forces with Lewis Weston Dillwyn's Cambrian Pottery, where Dillwyn experimented with several new formulae. However, in 1817, when he withdrew from the business, Billingsley and Young returned to reopen the Nantgarw factory. Although Billingsley left the factory in 1820 to take up a job at Coalport, Young managed to keep the business running for another two years along with Thomas Pardoe, a china painter from Bristol, as chief decorator.

Wares

Most Welsh porcelain consists of teawares or flatwares – dishes and plates – which were fired on spurs in a triangular arrangement of small iridescent circles. Large hollowares, such as ice pails, are extremely rare: many services had to be supplemented from other factories such as Paris.

Paste and glaze

Nantgarw porcelain is often heavier than Swansea's. It is very translucent and almost pure white when held up to a light. Nantgarw glaze is thick and smooth, with none of the rippling found on the later and thinner Swansea wares.

Swansea has at least three different types of porcelain, in which almost all extant examples are virtually flawless:

• duck egg, which is extremely thinly potted and has a decidedly green tone when in transmitted light

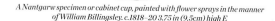

A Nantgarw specimen or cabinet cup, painted with flower sprays in the manner of William Billingsley. c.1818–20 3.75 in (9.5cm) high E

A Swansea cabinet cup and saucer, painted with Coningsburgh Castle. 1820 E

• the trident, which is named after its impressed mark, is smooth bodied but quite heavily potted

• the so-called glassy variety, which is very similar to contemporary Paris porcelain, with which it is often confused.

Decoration

Swansea wares were decorated by some of the best ceramic artists and gilders in Britain. The list includes Thomas Baxter, William Pollard and Henry Morris, as well as William Billingsley himself. The quality of their flower and landscape painting in particular had few equals.

Some Swansea porcelain and most Nantgarw porcelain was sent to London for decoration and sale at the top end of the market. The rest was decorated locally until 1823 at Nantgarw and 1826 at Swansea.

Most of the Nantgarw wares that were decorated in London have a faint border or iridescence around the painting, which was probably caused by a combination of both the different enamel mixtures and the different firing techniques used.

This cabinet cup and saucer (see right) is very typical of the pieces made at

Swansea. Exceptionally detailed flower painting, wild flowers, and fruit, especially the depiction of wild strawberries, dog roses, and speedwells, were a particular speciality of the factory's decorators. Morris had a neat and academic style, whereas the other great Swansea decorator, William Pollard, was considered to be more "romantic" and expansive. Pollard's plates will often have loose

A Swansea cabinet cup and saucer. c.1820 6in (15.5cm) high E

cuttings spread around the rim.

Marks

The Nantgarw mark, impressed in roman letters, is "NANT-GARW CW" (the "CW" stands for china works).

• Swansea marks are either impressed or stencilled; predominantly this would be in red enamel.

• There are some extremely dubious script Swansea marks around, often on plates that were actually made in Paris.

A Swansea lobed plate. c1820 8.5in (21.5cm) diam E

Vauxhall and Limehouse

*A Vauxhall Rococo
moulded cream boat,
adapted from a silver
shape. c.1760–5
5.5in (14cm) long D*

1. Is the porcelain soft-paste?

2. Has the unglazed porcelain burned brown in the firing?

3. Is the decoration a chinoiserie design with islands, pavillions, and
    pine trees or a bouquet of Meissen-style flowers painted in a lively
    palette?

4. Is the piece less than 8in (20.5cm) high?

5. If the piece is blue and white, is the blue inky or wet-looking?
    Vauxhall blue is often called "sticky blue".

6. Is the glaze on the blue and white wares patchy, with a strong
    greenish or bluish tone?

7. Does the porcelain body show small rips or tears under the glaze?

Vauxhall (c.1753–64)

After Chelsea and Bow, the most important of the London porcelain factories was the small Vauxhall China Works, set up by Nicholas Crisp in 1753, closing in 1764.

Wares

The factory mostly made teawares, "Goat and Bee" jugs, candlesticks, snuff boxes, and over 20 different forms of sauceboat.

Decoration

Bright polychrome enamels were used.

Paste and glaze

Using a soft-paste, on polychrome wares the glaze is creamy and opaque, but on blue and white wares it is bluish or greenish, becoming deep where pooled.

A Vauxhall chinoiserie leaf-shaped pickle dish. c.1758 3.75in (9.5cm) wide F

A Vauxhall vase, decorated with butterflies and caterpillars. c.1760 4.75in (12cm) high F

Limehouse (c.1745–48)

Although the least known of the London factories, Limehouse was a pioneer of English porcelain. Probably the first English factory to make blue and white porcelain, many wares previously ascribed to the Liverpool factories are now known to have been made at Limehouse. The output includes shell-shaped dishes, wavy-edged sauceboats with tripod feet shaped like lions' heads or cherubs, teapots, and chinoiserie pickle dishes. The earliest wares seem to have a pinkish tinge, but the later glaze is like a tin glaze.

A Limehouse porcelain blue and white figure, "The Old Viceroy of Kanton". c.1746 4.25in (11cm) high A

183

Longton Hall

A Longton Hall melon-shaped tureen, cover, and leaf-moulded stand. c.1755 9.5in (24cm) wide B

1. Is the porcelain soft-paste?
2. Is the piece heavily constructed?
3. Does it have firing cracks?
4. Has it collapsed slightly?
5. If a hollow figure, has it a smooth interior?
6. Is the surface of the piece greenish or greyish?
7. Is the glaze peppered with tiny black pinholes?
8. Are there broad washes of dark, runny underglaze blue?
9. Are tureens or plates moulded in the form of a leaf or a vegetable?

Longton Hall (1749–60)

The first of the famous Staffordshire factories was founded at Longton Hall in 1749 by a salt-glaze manufacturer, William Littler. During its short life, it made eccentric and slightly primitive wares and figures, which were often in shapes that showed the influence of salt-glaze stoneware.

Wares

The factory made mostly blue and white utilitarian wares, lively copies of Chinese *famille rose* patterns, and a famous range of fruit- and vegetable-shaped tureens and jugs, similar to those made at Chelsea and Worcester.

Paste and glaze

Longton Hall porcelain used a heavy soft-paste that is rather like Chelsea's. It has a surface that is quite often somewhat irregular.

The greyish glaze, containing tin, has been described by the great authority W. B. Honey as resembling paraffin wax.

A Longton Hall leaf dish with leaves and lilies. c.1755 9in (23cm) long E

Palette

The Longton Hall palette is unlike any other factory's and again shows the influence of salt-glaze wares. The most characteristic colours are:

- yellowish lime green
- pink
- crimson
- puce
- deep underglaze "Littler's Blue".

An early Longton Hall chinoiserie sparrow beak milk jug. c.1756 3.5in (9cm) high F

A Longton Hall basket, with pierced decoration. c.1749–60 9in (23cm) wide D

A pair of Longton Hall candlestick groups, in the form of two putti and a goat. c.1758 9in (23cm) high D

Designs

The sparrow beak jug (see p.185) dates from 1756 and is a very typical Longton Hall pattern.

These fine Rococo candlestick groups (see above) are typical of Longton Hall. The beautifully painted sprays of flowers are one of the reasons why Longton Hall wares are sometimes thought to have been made at Derby. Longton Hall is especially noted for slightly awkward *trompe l'oeil* fruit and vegetable tureens.

Although other factories made similar tureens, they did not give them spreading, leaf-shaped feet. Puce veining and pale edges on the leaves are also typical.

Figures

Both Longton Hall and Derby made very similar figures of "The Four Seasons". Among the figures that were produced, the "Four Continents" are considered the finest. But the two versions are not difficult to tell apart; these figures below display the slightly stiff postures and the doll-like faces that are much too simple to be Derby. Animal figures by Longton Hall are particularly collectable.

Marks

The Longton Hall mark consists of two reversed "L"s – standing for Littler and Longton – occasionally accompanied by one or more dots. On some pieces, these can look slightly like the crossed swords of Meissen. Although it is sometimes possible to find genuine pieces on which the Longton Hall mark

A Longton Hall figure of "Spring". c.1755 4.5in (11.5cm) high G

186

A Longton Hall turkey hen "snowman" candlestick figure. c.1758 D

A pair of Longton Hall pugs. c1755 3.5in (9cm) high C

has been impressed, it is far more likely that it was painted in underglaze blue.

West Pans

In 1760, financial problems forced Littler to close Longton Hall and sell out to William Duesbury of Derby. Littler moved to West Pans in Scotland, where he started another factory (1764–77). West Pans porcelain returned to the early paste and glaze used at Longton in the early 1750s. Almost all West Pans wares include decoration in "Littler's Blue", the distinctive, deep, and rather runny underglaze invented by Littler and subsequently used at both of his factories.

The first figures were heavily glazed and poorly defined white models of humans and animals, which have become known as "the snowman family". Later figures were slightly clumsy copies of Bow, Derby, or Meissen.

A pair of Longton Hall figures of an abbess and her novice. c.1755–60 5in (12.5cm) high F

Rockingham

A pair of Rockingham pot-pourri vases, painted in the style of John Creswell. c.1825 6.25in (16cm) high F

1. Is the porcelain hard-paste and ivory-coloured?
2. Does the glaze have very fine crazing?
3. If the piece is a plate, does it have a "C"-scroll border?
4. Has the colour sunk into the glaze?
5. Is the modelling of a much lower standard than the paste, the glaze, the palette, and the gilding?
6. Is the mark right?
7. If the piece is part of a service, does it have a pattern number either lower than 1559 or, if fractional, between 2/1 and 2/78?

Rockingham (1826–42)

In 1826, with the help of the considerable financial backing provided by their landlord, Earl Fitzwilliam, the Brameld family opened a porcelain factory at Swinton in Yorkshire and named it after the Marquis of Rockingham, from whom the Earl had inherited his estate. Ignoring utilitarian pieces, they then started to concentrate on ambitious products that were so sumptuous that they were seldom profitable. One of their most famous projects, the William IV dessert service, took seven years to make. In the end the pursuit of excellence ruined them, and the insolvent factory was forced to close in 1842.

Paste and glaze

Rockingham porcelain is warm, ivory-toned, and respected as a very high-quality hard-paste.
The glaze is sometimes blemished by crazing, which can be so fine that it is invisible to the naked eye.

Neo-rococo

Although Rockingham made a number of pieces in the Neo-classical style, it is best known for being at the forefront of the Neo-rococo revival. However, Rockingham wares are rare: many of the

A Rockingham vase and cover, with a gilt monkey finial. c.1830 25in (63.5cm) high E

elaborately moulded and flower-encrusted wares that are still attributed to the factory were in fact made by other English factories, which had followed Rockingham's example. This pot-pourri basket (see below), which is less than 4.25in (11cm) wide, epitomizes Rockingham's emphasis on modelling and surface decoration. The handle is made in the form of branches, foreshadowing the naturalism of the 1840s.

A Rockingham pot-pourri basket, encrusted with flowers and foliage. c.1830–42 4.25in (11cm) diam F

Rockingham figures

A Rockingham porcelain milkmaid, decorated in colour and gilt. c.1826–30 7in (18cm) high E

1. Is the paste of excellent quality?
2. Is it of a warm, ivory tone?
3. Is the glaze luminous?
4. Does the glaze have fine crazing?
5. Are the colours soft and muted?
6. Is the mark impressed rather than printed?

Rockingham figures

Rockingham figures were made only between 1826 and 1830. Although the modelling is not always of the highest standard, the quality of the paste, glaze, palette, and gilding make them generally superior to similar figures from Derby and Staffordshire. They are also sparingly decorated, and the colours are not so harsh.

Marks

From 1826 to 1830 the standard mark is the griffin from the Fitzwilliam crest over the words "Rockingham Works Brameld".
• A rarer version has "Rockingham Works" above the griffin and "Brameld" underneath.

A Rockingham porcelain model of a crouching hare. c.1826–42 2.5in (6.5cm) wide G

• After 1830 "Manufacturer to the King" was usually added. Rare versions for this period include "Royal Rockingham Brameld".
• On figures, the mark is usually impressed rather than printed.

A Rockingham porcelain peasant figure, "Paysanne de Sagran en Tirol". 1826–42 7.5in (19cm) high F

A Rockingham cat, wearing a gilt collar. c1830 2in (5.2cm) high F

191

Derby

*A documentary Derby shell-shaped pickle
dish. 1778 6.5in (16.5cm) wide F*

1. Is the porcelain soft-paste?
2. Is the paste fine-grained and greyish? (pre-1770)
3. Is the paste pure white? (post-1770)
4. Is the glaze greyish or slightly green? (pre-1770)
5. Is the glaze brilliant? (post-1770)
6. Is the gilding excellent?
7. Are there three patch marks in a triangle on the base? (post-1756)

Derby (1750–1848)

The Derby factory was founded in 1750 by a Frenchman, André Planché. In 1756, it was bought out by John Heath and his partner William Duesbury, who had until then been decorating pieces for Chelsea. In 1770, they also bought the Chelsea factory, and for the next 14 years, in a phase known as Chelsea-Derby, the two concerns operated together. In 1811, the business was acquired from Heath and Duesbury's successors by Robert Bloor, who, despite the fact that he had a mental breakdown in 1826, continued to manage the declining factory with his children until it closed in 1848. Several other factories were established in Derby in the 19thC. The most successful of these was the so-called "Crown Derby" company, which still survives

A Derby porcelain jug. c.1780
9in (23cm) high G

today as the Royal Crown Derby Porcelain Company.

Paste and glaze

The earliest Derby soft-paste is fine-grained and greyish and has almost the appearance of hard-paste, even in conchoidal fractures.

• The early glaze is greyish white, or sometimes greyish green. Often, there are tiny pinprick flecks in it.

• Pieces made after the arrival of Duesbury in 1756 have a more refined appearance. Although the paste is still the same, the glaze, which can still be slightly green, is much thinner and also more translucent.

• After the acquisition of the Chelsea

A Derby leaf-moulded dish. c.1760–5
6.5in (16.5cm) wide G

A Derby cabinet cup and trembleuse *saucer, painted by James Banford.*
c.1790 D

factory in 1770, the paste and glaze improved to become some of the best in England. The porcelain that Derby made in the last years of the 18thC is pure and quite white, and the glaze is brilliant and bluish.

Wares

At first almost all the Derby products were figures. Until the introduction of a new formula in 1770, the porcelain tended to split on exposure to boiling water. As a result early tea and coffee wares are extremely rare.

• After 1756, all products were fired on pads of clay, which left a triangle of greyish patch marks on the bases.

• The majority of early wares were left in the white, and the remainder were decorated in pale enamel. After 1756 the colours became brighter and clearer.

Underglaze blue

The very rare blue and white wares from Derby are invariably decorated with chinoiserie and cell diaper, or trellis borders in a slight grey underglaze cobalt.

Designs

After 1770, the quality of design at Derby improved considerably. The leading landscape painters at the factory during this period were Zachariah Boreman and George Robertson. The Derby porcelain factory specialized in this type of finely painted cabinet cup in the 1790s (see left). Such cabinet pieces were mainly intended for display and were valued as small-scale

This mark c.1782–1825
In red c.1806–25

A pair of early 19thC Derby vases, decorated by William "Quaker" Pegg. 12.75in (32.5cm) high B

Chelsea and Worcester, made vessels with moulded ribbing, they did not end it so far from the rim.

• Derby specialized in high-quality painting, often of exotic birds, which were loosely painted copies of Chelsea red-anchor designs, which were in turn copied from Sèvres. But by the 1770s Chelsea was making gold-anchor wares with copious gilding.

• "Rope-twist" handles and applied flowers at terminals and intersections were used by several factories, but Derby tended to use two colours instead of one to decorate the handles, and its flowers are on a slightly larger scale, with centres that look like hollow tubes.

Isleworth (c.1760–1800)
A small number of "Derby" underglaze blue wares have been reattributed to Isleworth following a dig on site in 1997. The Isleworth Porcelain factory was established by Joseph Shore, who came to Isleworth probably from Worcester in 1757. It made tea and dinner wares in blue painted and printed designs, similar to Derby and Lowestoft wares of the period. The factory closed in 1831.

works of art. They were rarely, if ever, used. The Derby pattern books indicate that James Banford was to paint the medallions on cups with this border pattern. The leading botanical painters were William ("Quaker") Pegg and William Billingsley. The exquisite vases above were painted with finely detailed flowers by "Quaker" Pegg. The quality of the gilding is exceptional. The Derby gilders inherited Chelsea's mantle as the best in Britain, and often demonstrated their skill by gilding each piece in a service with a different border. Gilders are identified by a number. Then, in the 1770s, Derby became the first English factory to introduce pattern numbers. Although other factories, including

Derby figures

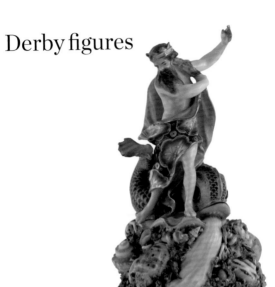

*A Derby model of
Neptune. c.1758–65
9.75in (25cm) high G*

1. Is the figure dry-edged (see opposite)?
2. Is it decorated in a subdued palette in which turquoise, pink, and iron red predominate? (pre-1811)
3. Is the figure over-decorated? (post-1811)
4. Is the base integrated with the figure?
5. Are the paste and the glaze right (see pp.193–4)?
6. Is the mark right (see pp.194 and 199)?
7. Are there patch marks on the base (see p.194)?

Early figures

It has been suggested that Duesbury encouraged Planché (see p.193) to make figures because he could not get enough from Chelsea for his workshops to decorate.

However, the earliest Derby figures are of a much lower standard than the Chelsea products.

With the usual range of pastoral and allegorical subjects, they are stiffly modelled – although this may be due to the over-plasticity of the clay – and they stand on simple bases that are quite similar to those on the early Meissen figures of Kändler.

Fortunately, most of them have been left in the white. The few that have been decorated are primitive. For example, the mouths so badly painted that the lips look misshapen.

Before 1756, the glutinous glaze was wiped away from the edge of the base in order to prevent it from sticking the figure to the supports in the kiln during the firing. As a result, the figures from this period are known as "Dry-edge Derby".

Early Duesbury-period figures

Throughout the early years of Duesbury's management, the modellers at Derby

A Derby dry-edge figure of "Columbine". c.1753 5in (12.5cm) high E

A Derby figure of a child harlequin. c.1760 4.5in (11.5cm) high E

A Derby group adorning a bust of Pan. c.1780 13.5in (34cm) high F

A pair of Derby models of parrots.
c.1755 5.5in (14cm) high C

In the last quarter of the 18thC, when taste changed from the Rococo to Neo-classicism, Derby followed the example of many European factories and produced some fine biscuit figures. Modelled by Pierre Stephan, William Coffee, and J. J. Spengler, the son of the director of the Zürich factory, these elegant and detailed figures are among the best products of Derby, and are seriously undervalued today.

• The influence of Tournai and other Continental factories is evident in the very architectural nature of the

were still constrained by the weakness of the clay, but their figures are much livelier and have a greater subtlety and grace about them. Many of them look as though they have just got up from a comfortable chair and are stretching their long limbs.

Like the mythological figure in the main picture (see p.196), they stand on elaborate bases that integrate completely with the figures. This feature is quite unlike the products of any other English factory.

Their clothes are covered in neat, delicate, and lightly painted flowers, and they are also decorated in a fairly subdued palette in which the dominant colours are often turquoise, pink, and iron red.

A Derby boar, naturalistically decorated in brown and black. c.1755 2.5in (6.5cm) high E

A pair of Derby stags, decorated in iron red and manganese. c.1760 7.25in (18.5cm) high E

rockwork, as well as in the circular order of the factory's figures.

Bloor figures

Under Bloor (see p.193) the quality of the factory's figures declined. Most figures were overdecorated, with heavily rouged cheeks, sombre colours, and square, octagonal or even debased Rococo bases.

Marks

Derby wares and figures were not marked until the acquisition of Chelsea in 1770. From 1770 to 1784 various combinations of the anchor and the letter "D" were used, usually in gilding. However, the commonest mark is a crown over a "D". From 1782 until 1825, the mark was a crown over crossed batons and a "D" with three dots either side

of the batons. Before 1806 the usual colours were puce or blue. After that red was used exclusively.

A Derby ram, naturalistically decorated in brown. c.1760–65 4.5in (11.5cm) wide F

American porcelain

From their earliest days, American porcelain manufacturers had to struggle against competition from England, Continental Europe and the Far East, which the American public usually perceived as superior. This meant that few American ceramics firms enjoyed widespread commercial success, especially during the boom periods of production in Europe. The history of American porcelain is closely linked to the skills of immigrant potters. The first commercial manufacturer of American porcelain was the American China Manufactory of Bonnin & Morris (see pp. 202–3), which survived for only two years. No significant manufacturer of porcelain operated in the United States for over 40 years after Bonnin & Morris's well-publicized failure. But by the 1820s, porcelain in the fashionable French taste was being made and decorated in small factories throughout the North-East. The best known of these firms was William Ellis Tucker (see pp.204-7) in Philadelphia, which was in operation from 1825 until 1838. Unlike most earlier American wares, which show the distinct influence of either English or French taste, Tucker porcelains combine European forms and materials with American proportions and motifs.

The heavy immigration from Europe into the United States during the 1840s provided new talents for the potting trade and a greatly expanded domestic market. Porcelain factories were established in Ohio, Vermont, New Jersey, and New York City, where there was a concentration of factories in the Greenpoint section of Brooklyn. This group included Charles Cartlidge's pottery (see p.207). An

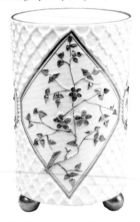

A Belleek Lotus ware vase, by Knowles, Taylor & Knowles. c.1892–1900 7.75in (19.5cm) high G

An Ott and Brewer cup and saucer. 1885 5.5in (14cm) diam G

immigrant from Staffordshire, and a former agent for William Ridgway, who began making porcelain in c.1848, Cartlidge concentrated on decorative hollowwares and an extensive variety of dust-pressed items from buttons to door plaques. Although it closed after eight years, his pottery was the model for a neighbouring factory, which operated as the Union Porcelain Works from 1861 until 1910. This factory produced some of the most innovative designs in American porcelain.

The Philadelphia Centennial Exhibition of 1876 gave American porcelain manufacturers a new awareness of the supremacy of overseas competition, particularly from England, France, and Japan. But apart from the works established by Ott and Brewer in Trenton, New Jersey, in the mid-1860s, few firms could meet the competition on an equal footing. The Ott and Brewer Works used Parian porcelain for high-standard sculptural and hollowware, and in the post-Centennial period it made an ivory-coloured porcelain body for expensive decorative wares. During the last quarter of the 19thC, Ott and Brewer was also prominent among American manufacturers of extremely thin and intricately formed eggshell porcelain in the style of the Irish Belleek factory. All decorative American eggshell or "eggshell type" porcelain, most of which was made in the Trenton area, is known collectively as American Belleek. The best exponent of American Belleek was the factory established in Trenton in 1889 by Walter Scott Lenox.

Bonnin & Morris

A rare Bonnin & Morris pickle stand/sweetmeat dish. 1770–72 5.5in (14cm) high A

1. Is the item relatively thickly potted?
2. Is the glaze uneven, pitted, and bubbled?
3. Are unglazed areas stained a brownish colour?
4. Is the paste "porridgy" and barely translucent?
5. Is moulded ornament, florettes in particular, relatively crudely fashioned?
6. Are painted landscapes unlike those found on contemporary English blue and white porcelain?

The American China Manufactory (1770–72)

This shortlived porcelain firm was founded by Gousse Bonnin and George Anthony Morris in the Southwark district of Philadelphia. It was the first of its kind in the United States but it failed within 18 months of opening, mainly because neither Bonnin nor Morris had any experience of the ceramics trade, nor access to a successful porcelain formula. Also, they relied on the support of local patrons who baulked at paying up to five times the cost of comparable, imported items. The workforce included nine "master workers" whom Bonnin enticed to Philadelphia from England.

Types of wares

By the spring of 1771 Bonnin & Morris offered a complete range of tablewares, including full tea and dinner services, cups and teabowls, sauceboats, "dressing boxes", openwork baskets, pickle dishes, and sweetmeat stands. The factory used American clays mixed with calcined animal bones for its porcelain body, which is of a soft-paste type. Most extant pieces are thickly potted. The paste tends to be "porridgy" and may not show translucence except under strong light, when a brownish colour and "moons" are present. Unglazed body areas tend to turn yellowish brown and the glaze is usually pitted or bubbled, showing pools of a greenish-blue tint.

Decoration

The documented pieces by this factory are blue and white, most of them painted in a bold style. Painted motifs include conventional diapered borders, chinoiseries, flowers, and landscapes, which sometimes combine English river scenes with Dutch-style buildings. At the beginning of 1771 Bonnin & Morris appealed to the Assembly in Philadelphia for a loan and ran a lottery in New Castle, Delaware "for the encouragement of the American China Manufactory", but to no avail. By the end of the following year they had closed their factory and were appealing again, this time for charity, on behalf of the now unemployed craftsmen who had been brought over from England. However, the appeal failed and the factory was forced to closed for good.

A rare Bonnin & Morris soft-paste sauceboat. 1770–72 2.25in (6cm) high A

William Ellis Tucker

A Tucker "Grecian" pitcher. 1832–8 7.25in (18.5cm) high D

1. Is the porcelain extremely white and heavy?
2. Is the floral painting of similar style and standard to that found on contemporary English porcelain?
3. Are painted scenes uniquely American?
4. Is the enamel palette comparable to contemporary Paris porcelain?
5. Is the landscape painting comparatively crudely drawn and with a naïve quality?
6. Is the gilding profuse and subject to rubbing?

William Ellis Tucker (1826–38)

Tucker was a wealthy Philadelphian whose factory used clays from Delaware, Pennsylvania, New York, and New Jersey as well as refined materials from the failed works of Ducasse and Chanou in New York City. Tucker employed at least two partners. After his premature death in 1832, the business was carried on by his younger brother, Thomas Tucker. Tucker's factory was the largest American porcelain manufactury in the first half of the 19thC.

Two Tucker jugs, with decorated grisaille landscapes. c.1825 9.5in (24cm) high G

A gilt-decorated Tucker and Hemphill footed basket. c.1830 8.5in (21.5cm) high F

Types of ware

Tucker's earliest recorded wares were milk jugs, known in the United States as "china pitchers", and throughout the factory's history, pitchers of all kinds were among its most successful products.

By 1830, Tucker's output included ornamental and spill vases, 12 pitchers, pierced fruit stands, teawares, a night light, butter dishes, plates, bowls, covered dishes, compotes, and a "spitting box and a funnel".

• Tucker porcelain is not as scarce as pieces by Bonnin & Morris (see pp.202–3), but it is rarely seen on the market.

• Collectors favour interesting forms and polychrome-decorated examples, especially those with motifs of American interest, and marked pieces.

*A Tucker and Hemphill porcelain pitcher,
decorated with the Philadelphia Waterworks
and the Upper Ferry Bridge. 1826–32
8in (20.5cm) high E*

• The bodies of Tucker wares are usually
very white and glassy.

Designs

Most of Tucker's porcelain is French
in taste, although English forms were
also followed. French models include
"Empire" vases and Paris-style useful
wares. Most pieces are distinguishable
from European wares by their
exaggerated proportions.

Decoration

While some of Tucker's products were
only sparsely gilded or monogrammed,

much of the ware was heavily coated
in gilt, which is quite easily rubbed
away. The decorative schemes often
included simple painted landscapes in
sepia or black. Polychrome decoration
is limited to floral compositions of
variable quality, which are notably
similar to English Coalport wares, and
American scenes or landscapes. Some
of these are extremely naïve and may be
the work of William Tucker's younger
brother Thomas.

*A Tucker and Hemphill pitcher, decorated by
Charles J. Boulter. 1826–32
12in (30.5cm) high D*

No transfer-printed ware is known, and the paste, enamels, and gilding closely resemble that used in contemporary Paris.

Marks

Although most Tucker porcelain was unmarked, some pieces carry the maker's name or "PHILAD" painted in red. The names of Tucker's two known financial partners also occasionally appeared on the marks.

Charles Cartlidge and Co. (1848–56)

Charles Cartlidge was a potter from Staffordshire who emigrated to New York in 1832. After working as an agent for William Ridgway's English pottery, he set up his own soft-paste factory in Greenpoint, Brooklyn, in 1848. Five years later, when his products had won a prize for quality, he had four large kilns and employed 60 people.

The Cartlidge factory made a large number of moulded pitchers in several sizes. The most common moulded decorations are an oak-leaf motif and corn stalks, such as those on this example (see above right), c.1850.

• Other typical wares include "porcelain tea, table and fancy wares", most of which were slipcast and finished in gilt, or small dust-pressed items, such as buttons.

• Cartlidge paste is similar to contemporary English bone china and

A mid-19thC pitcher decorated with an American eagle and shield, by Charles Cartlidge and Co. 10in (25.5cm) high E

is usually thickly potted.

• Most Cartlidge pieces have gilt decoration and monograms are especially common.

• Cartlidge is sometimes marked "American Porcelain" painted in gilt script, but most pieces are unmarked.

• Signed wares and those painted with polychrome American motifs, are very sought after.

The Union Porcelain Co.

A rare vase, designed by Karl Mueller, with busts of George Washington. 12.75in (32.5cm) high B

1. Is the modelling comparatively crude?
2. Is the ware thinly potted and brittle?
3. Does the finish appear smear-glazed and the enamel painting semi-matt?
4. Is the palette pale and muted?
5. Is the gilding poor and subject to rubbing?
6. Are the ornamental motifs exotic and in extraordinary combinations?

The Union Porcelain Co. (1850–1910)

In 1884 William, Anthony, and Francis Victor Boch founded a pottery on Fifth Street in the Greenpoint section of Brooklyn. The brothers' works was comparable to that operated by the neighbouring factory of Charles Cartlidge (see p.207), and some moulded pitchers have been attributed to either. In 1861, the firm was purchased by Thomas Carl Smith, who renamed the company the Union Porcelain Co. (later called the Union Porcelain Works).

Designs

This moulded porcelain ice pitcher (see below), designed by Karl L. H. Mueller, is known as the "Uncle Sam" pitcher.

A Union Porcelain Works oyster plate. c.1885 9.5in (24cm) G

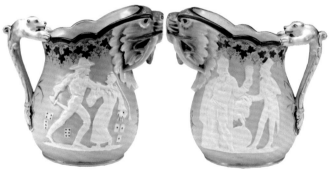

The "Uncle Sam" pitcher, designed by Karl L. H. Mueller. 9.75in (25cm) high C

An Union Porcelain Works exceptional large urn. 20.5in (52cm) high D

It has various patriotic and contemporary references – the walrus spout and polar bear handle, and relief figures of King Gambrinus, the Norse God of beer, offering a drink to Brother Jonathan, a character from Royall Tyler's comedy, *The Contrast*, who came to symbolize America and Uncle Sam. The reverse has a fight scene between

Bill Nye and Chinese Gamber Ah Sin, who were popular characters of the time.

Wares

Like Cartlidge, the Boch brothers made extensive use of Prosser's dust-pressing patent in the manufacturing of porcelain sundries. The products included name plates and door plaques, but useful hollowares were the factory's main focus.

For most of its existence, the Union Porcelain Works was operated by Charles H. L. Smith, son of the founder, who expanded its output in the 1860s to include decorative tablewares, such as oyster plates. These were made in a white, glassy porcelain and usually finished in lustrous, coloured glazes.

Designs

In the early 1870s Karl Muller, a German-born sculptor, served as art director of the Union Porcelain Works. Muller was responsible for the extraordinary, sculptured designs that were produced at the works from c.1875, including the famous Century Vase made for the Philadelphia Centennial exhibition of 1876. The vase was made in a small size (12in/30.5cm), and some examples are signed with "K. MULLER" on the moulded relief portrait of George Washington. Under Muller's direction, the company's product range expanded to include decorative tablewares with exotic moulded ornament such as the "Heathen-Chinee" pitcher, probably designed in 1875, moulded with a figural scene from a contemporary poem. This Union Porcelain "Liberty cup" (see below), modelled by Muller, ranks with his "Century Vase" among the most famous pieces in the history of American porcelain.

Muller trained as a clay sculptor in Paris, and the French influence is particularly evident here in the cup's Neo-rococo foot, and, of course, in the figures of Liberty. These cups are sometimes gilded.

A "Liberty" cup and saucer, Karl L. H. Mueller. c.1876 F

Decoration

Muller's repertoire of motifs includes mandarin head-finials, handles shaped like polar bears and other animals, and feet modelled as rabbits.

The wares were often decorated with relief-moulded figures, and they were usually painted in a muted palette and were always extensively gilded. The models of animals are usually realistically coloured. The inspiration for this category of Union Porcelain, which is by far the most collectable and rare, includes Egyptian, Chinese, Japanese, and American historical motifs as well as flora and fauna. Many of these have a Parian-type body with a high or smear glaze.

As well as being the first American factory to make a true, hard-paste porcelain, the Union Porcelain Works was the first factory to employ underglaze colours.

Marks

Few examples of Boch porcelain are marked, although some pitchers moulded with Bacchanalian motifs have an impressed signature. Union Porcelain Works marks include the incised initials "U.P.W." as well as the full factory name painted or stamped and the initials "N.Y." (for New York) or "L.I." (for Long Island).

Copies and fakes

Most porcelain fakes and forgeries were produced in the 20thC, but the business of copying porcelain has an ancient and much more honourable tradition. During the 18thC the Chinese potters were still following 14thC designs, and inscribing them with earlier, Classical reign marks, not with any intention to deceive, but out of respect for the artistry of their predecessors.

In Paris during the late 19thC, the famous Samson factory made many copies of both Oriental and European porcelain, but once again there was seldom any obvious intention to deceive. Most of the pieces carried the factory's "S" mark, and the rest were usually betrayed by other means.

A pair of early 20thC Chelsea-style porcelain figures, modelled as a seated gentleman and a lady, he with a dog at his feet, she with a sheep, gold anchor mark. 7.5in (19cm) high H

A set of four late 19thC Samson "Meissen" figures of gods, marks in blue. 6in (15.5cm) high H

Some of the earliest forgeries, were the mid-18thC French and English copies, which were deceptively inscribed with the prestigious marks of Sèvres and Meissen. Faking, in which pieces were altered to look like something rarer and more valuable, can be said to have started in the late 18thC, when large numbers of Sèvres pieces were bought in the white by independent decorators who painted them in the Sèvres style and inscribed them with its mark. In the 21stC, when "investment collecting" led to escalating prices, factories were set up all over the Far East to imitate old Oriental wares; some

dealers simply removed the "S" from Samson pieces, and in China the finest fakers of all took genuine but mundane Ming pieces, stripped them with acid, and redecorated them with rare designs. Some copies, especially those by Samson, are collectable, particularly larger scale wares, and Imari or *famille rose*-type figures.

American porcelain is seldom copied or faked. When assessing a piece of porcelain it is important to check the paste, the glaze, the enamels used, and any distinguishing features before believing a mark. If something looks too good to be true it probably is!

German ceramics

A late 19thC German Meissen-style inkwell, incised "Y38 6", stamped "29". 2.75in (7cm) diam H

Most German fakes and forgeries were intended to be mistaken for 18thC Meissen. Throughout the 19thC, many German factories continued to make copies of 18thC Meissen products and to inscribe them with similar to identical marks. They were so popular that even Meissen made copies, which were at least better than the others. During the 18thC, Meissen wares were faked by several minor factories in Thuringia, where they were inscribed with spurious crossed swords marks. They were also imitated in England. For example, the Derby factory used Chinese Meissen wares as models; and in c.1755 the Chelsea factory copied a whole consignment of Meissen wares and figures. During the 19thC, a considerable number of factories produced excellent imitations of Meissen. One of the best was Carl

Thieme's factory in Potschappel, and another was the Dresden factory of Helena Wolfsohn, who copied Meissen wares of the 1740s and even added the Augustus Rex mark, until Meissen obtained an injunction against her, forcing her to change the mark to a crown above the word "Dresden".

The "Meissen hoopoes" were made by Edmé Samson of Paris, who started his career in 1845 as a decorator of white porcelains from other factories. In the 1850s he set up a hard-paste factory in Montreuil and began to make his own porcelain copies. The use of colour is on the whole insensitive compared with the originals. A close look at the unglazed areas on both pieces reveals the smooth greyish paste of the Samson factory, which is not at all like the dirty, gouged surface on most genuine Meissen footrims.

Early Meissen figures are meticulously decorated. The hair in particular is very finely detailed. The thick brushstrokes that Samson's painters have used would only be found on 19thC Meissen. Samson's surface is relatively smooth compared with Meissen's, and his glaze is much glassier. However, the most obvious differences are in the base: Samson's painters have not quite captured the yellowish-green foliage that typifies early Meissen. Also, Meissen bases are often quite sharp-edged, whereas Samson's tend to be subtly rounded.

A Meissen-style porcelain mantel clock, modelled as a chariot with two cherubs and two goats (some restoration). 15.5in (39cm) G

A pair of early 20thC Samson "Meissen" hoopoes, pseudo crossed swords marks. 11.25in (28.5cm) high H

French ceramics

A late 19thC German cabinet cup and saucer. c.1910-20 5.25in (13cm) diam H

Sèvres

Ever since the French royal factory moved from Vincennes to Sèvres, in 1756, its porcelain has been copied and faked by almost every European factory. When the factory was founded, its declared purpose was to make porcelain in the manner of Meissen, but remarkably 15 years later the roles were reversed and even Meissen was copying the styles of Sèvres.

Very few of the early copies were made with any intention to deceive, and almost all of them are easy to detect.

But after the French Revolution many white wares were sold off to outside decorators in England as well as France and on many of these the enamelling is so effective that it has even deceived experts. Some later-decorated pieces are very fine and currently undervalued. In England the fashion for Sèvres never died out. In 1813 the new Nantgarw factory produced moulded wares in Sèvres' old Rococo style.

By the middle of the century Coalport and Minton were making accurate copies of the large decorative pieces

A pair of French vases in the Sèvres style, probably Samson. 6.5in (16.5cm) high G

that Sèvres had made a hundred years earlier, and Minton was actually using a Sèvres mark.

Most fakes are made of hard-paste porcelain and not soft-paste like Sèvres.

• Although most Sèvres are marked with interlaced "L"s, very few have date letters like the originals.

• Sèvres had very stringent quality controls. If the piece has the slightest flaw, the best it can be is a reject that has been decorated later.

• The gilding on Sèvres copies and fakes is often brassy and flat, and it is very seldom up to the standard of the original, that was the best.

Other factories

At the end of the 19thC and the beginning of the 20thC, a number of Paris hard-paste factories produced copies of Chantilly, Saint-Cloud and other early soft-paste wares.

By far the best were made by Emil Samson, the son of Edmé, but, like all the others, he was betrayed by his paste. The Saint-Cloud factory produced some of the loveliest porcelain in France with a warm, creamy glaze. As he could not use a soft paste, Emil Samson attempted to reproduce it here in a *faïence* fine. However, faïence is very difficult to pot neatly. The result was a mixture of granular body, inaccurate potting, and also clumsily applied flowers.

A fake Sèvres mark

A Sèvres-style French porcelain gilt-metal-mounted, two-handled oval centre bowl late 19thC. 18in (45cm) wide H

English ceramics

A late 19thC Samson assembled garniture, in the Worcester manner, comprising three vases and covers, each of hexagonal form. F

Worcester

The Japanese patterns of Worcester have always been popular with copyists, especially in Paris. There are large numbers of scale-blue wares with spurious seal marks in circulation. However, these are simple to detect, as Worcester's soapstone porcelain has a distinctive grainy and greyish look, while the copies are almost always slick and glassy.

• There are fewer copies and fakes of the wares decorated by James Giles.

• During the 19thC Worcester made many hard-paste wares.

• Even today a number of copyists

A pair of second late19thC marks, minor damages. 12.5in (32cm) high H

are producing hard-paste versions of Worcester blue and white wares. The Booth's factory in Tunstall made a large number of reproductions of Worcester scale-blue wares. They were inscribed with the factory's mark, but even without this there are

several reasons why they are unlikely to be mistaken for the originals:

• They are made of fine earthenware, which is slightly brown.

• The designs are transfer-printed, which makes them rather dull and lifeless.

• The proportions are all wrong.

Bow

There are relatively few copies of Bow porcelain. Samson and the other French copyists tended to ignore the factory, although it did not escape the attentions of Reginald Newland and one or two other unknown artists.

Derby

Only a few Derby pieces were copied, but they were copied quite often and by many different copyists. There are a number of English country houses that contain one of Samson's versions of the frill vase.

A pair of Samson "Derby gold anchor" figures of Turks. 9.5in (24cm) high H

An early 19thC porcelain cabinet cup and saucer, possibly Samson. 6in (15.5cm) wide H

Glossary

baluster double curved form that swells at the base and rises in a concave curve to a narrow stem or neck.

Baroque extravagant, and heavily ornate style of decoration that originated in 17thC Italy. Meissen's porcelain of the early 18thC is the most notable.

basketweave decorative relief pattern resembling woven willow or cane; applied to the borders of plates and dishes.

bat printing a type of transfer-printing used by early 19thC Staffordshire factories. The design would be transferred from an engraved plate to a glazed surface via slabs of glue or gelatin (bats).

bisque unglazed porcelain or earthenware fired once only. Popular for Neo-classical porcelain figures.

blanc de Chine translucent white Chinese porcelain, unpainted and with a thick glaze. It was made at kilns in Dehua in the Fujian province from the Song Dynasty and copied in Europe.

blue and white white Oriental or Western ceramics with painted or printed cobalt-blue enamel decoration.

bocage French term for trees or foliage in the form of an arbour surrounding or supporting a pottery or porcelain figure.

bone-ash burnt, crushed animal bone that is added to soft paste porcelain mixture to fuse the ingredients. The process was introduced c.1750 at Bow and other English factories.

bone china soft-paste porcelain consisting of petuntse (china stone), kaolin (china clay), and dried bone. Supposedly invented by Josiah Spode II in c.1794, it became the mainstay of the English porcelain industry from c.1820.

bracket lobes bracket-shaped moulding used on dish rims.

cachepot ornamental container for flower-pots. A smaller version of jardinière.

caillouté ("pebbled") irregular pattern of meshed ovals, usually gilded, that resemble pebbles and used on some Sèvres porcelain.

campana vase an inverted, bell-shaped vase sometimes with a handle on each shoulder).

cartouche decorative motif in the form of a scroll of paper with rolled ends, bearing a picture, motif, or monogram. Also used to describe a frame, usually oval, decorated with scrollwork.

celadon semi-opaque, green-tinted glaze used first during the Chinese Song Dynasty.

chinoiserie Oriental-style decoration that permeated Europe from the late 17thC.

crazing tiny surface cracks caused by shrinking or other technical defects in a glaze.

delftware/Delftware tin-glazed earthenware made in Delft in the Netherlands. Refers to British ware when it does not have a capital letter.

diaper decorative pattern of repeated diamonds or other geometrical shapes.

documentary wares that bear evidence indicating the origin of the piece, such as the signature of the decorator or modeller, or an armorial mark.

dry-edge an unglazed area around the base of some early Derby figures.

earthenware term for a type of pottery, which is porous and requires a glaze.

en camaïeu painted decoration in different tones of one colour.

enamel form of decoration involving the application of metallic oxides to metal, ceramics, or glass in paste form or in an oil-based mixture, which is then usually fired for decorative effect.

faïence French term for tin-glazed earthenware.

feldspar a rock-forming mineral (also known as Chinese petuntse) used to make hard-paste porcelain. Feldspar china, a variant of bone china, was made from c.1820.

fêtes galantes open-air scenes of aristocratic amusement that were a favourite theme of French Rococo painters.

firing process of baking ceramics in a kiln. Temperatures range from 800° to 1100°C (1500-2000°F) for earthenware to 14000°C (2550°F) for the second firing of hard-paste porcelain and stoneware.

fluting pattern of concave grooves repeated in vertical, parallel lines. The opposite of gadrooning.

gadrooning decorative edging consisting of a series of convex, vertical, or spiralling curves.

gilding a decorative process whereby patterns are etched into porcelain with hydrofluoric acid, then gilded and burnished.

hard-paste porcelain the technical term for porcelain made according to the Chinese formula, also known as true porcelain. It was first made using the combination of kaolin (china clay: 50%), petuntse (china stone: 25%), and quartz (25%).

Imari Japanese porcelain with dense decoration, based on brocade patterns, in a palette that is dominated by underglaze blue, iron red, green, manganese, yellow, and gold.

Japonaise (also Japonaiserie) term used to describe European designs, c.1862 to 1900, inspired by Japanese art.

Kakiemon type of Japanese porcelain named after a family of potters, who may have introduced it in the Arita district of Japan during the 17thC. Designs are often asymmetrical in a palette of iron-red, cerulean-blue, turquoise green, yellow, aubergine, and gold.

Kaolin (china clay) fine, white granite clay used to make hard-paste porcelain.

knop decorative knobs on lids and covers or the projection or bulge in the stem of a glass or candlestick.

Laub und Bandelwerk (leaf and strapwork) decoration of interwoven leaves and strapwork, often surrounding a cartouche. Most popular during the 18thC.

majolica corruption of the term maiolica, which refers to a type of 19thC earthenware in elaborate forms with thick, brightly coloured running glazes.

moons air bubbles in porcelain paste that expand during firing, leaving translucent spots.

moulding relief decoration made separately from the body and applied later.

mount a decorative ormolu or gilt-bronze attachment to porcelain.

Neo-classical mid-to late-18thC style of architecture and decoration based on the forms of ancient Greece and Rome. Elements include garlands of flowers, palmettes, husks, vases, urns, key patterns, and mythical creatures.

oeil de perdrix literally "eye of a partridge"; a pattern of dotted circles in enamel or gilding; introduced at the Sèvres porcelain factory from the late 1760s and later copied by the Meissen and other factories.

ormolu ("gilt bronze") gilded, brass-like alloy of copper, zinc, and tin, used for mounts on fine furniture.

Parian semi-matt porcelain made with feldspar and therefore not requiring a separate glaze. Also called "statuary porcelain", it became known as Parian because of its similarity to the white marble from the Greek island of Paros.

petuntse (china stone) a fusable, feldspathic bonding mineral essential for making hard-paste porcelain or bone china.

press moulding technique involving pouring molten glass into a metal mould and pressing it to the sides using a metal plunger. Also refers to the moulding of applied ornament by pressing clay into an absorbent mould.

puce purple red colour formed from manganese oxide.

quatrefoil shape or design incorporating four foils or lobes.

Rococo decorative style that evolved in the early 18thC partly as a reaction to the Baroque. It featured asymmetrical ornament and flamboyant scrollwork.

rose Pompadour deep-pink glaze introduced at Sèvres as a ground colour.

salt-glaze thin, glassy glaze applied to some stoneware and produced by throwing salt into the kiln at the height of firing. The glaze may show a pitted surface, known as "orange peel".

Schwarzlot German term for black lead enamel painting on porcelain and glass used from the second half of the 17thC.

slipcasting manufacture of thin-bodied ceramic wares and figures by pouring slip into a mould.

soft-paste porcelain (artificial porcelain) porcelain formula which may include soapstone or bone-ash, but without the kaolin used in hard-paste porcelain.

spur mark small defects on the base or footrim of a piece made by the supporting stilts (or cockspurs) used during firing.

stoneware type of pottery fired at a higher temperature than earthenware, making it durable and non-porous. May be covered in a salt-glaze.

sumptuary laws laws forbidding the import, ownership, or manufacture of luxury goods.

tin glaze glassy glaze made opaque by the addition of tin oxide and commonly used on earthenware.

transfer-printing transfer of an inked image from an engraved plate to paper or to a sheet ("bat") of tacky glue and from there to a ceramic object.

trembleuse French term for a saucer with a raised ring to hold a cup to avoid spillages.

underglaze colour or design painted before the application of the glaze on a ceramic object. Blue is the most common underglaze colour.

wreathing spiralling indented rings inside thrown pottery, left by the potter's fingers, or caused by distortions during the firing process.

Index

Page number in *italic*
refer to the illustrations.

232

Acknowledgements

Albert Amor
37 Bury Street, St James's,
London SW1Y 6AU
www.albertamor.co.uk
*p.7, p.10, p.19, p.27, p.110bc, p.124,
p.128, p.129bc, p.135tc, p.136,
p.137cr, p.140, p.151bl, p.152bl,
p.156, p.157cr, p.157bl, p.183bl,
p.184, p.185tr, p.186tl, p.187tr,
p.197tl, p.197br, p.198br, p.199tc*

Alfies Antiques Market
13-25 Church Street,
London NW8 8DT
p.216, p.217bl

Matthew Barton Ltd
25 Blythe Road London
W14 0PD
www.matthewbartonltd.com
p.116

Auktionshaus Bergmann
Möhrendorferstraße 4,
91056 Erlangen, Germany
*p.35cr, p.37br, p.37br, p.57br,
p.58, p.61br, p.64, p.65tr, p.67cr,
p.69tr, p.74, p.79tr, p.81bl,
p.82bc, p.83tl, p.84, p.89bl*

**Bearnes Hampton and
Littlewood**
St Edmund's Court
Okehampton Street,
Exeter, Devon EX4 1DU
www.bearnes.co.uk
*p.13br, p.78, p.154br, p.172,
p.173bl, p.177tr, p.177bc*

Bloomsbury Auctions
Bloomsbury House,
24 Maddox Street, London
W1S 1PP
p.214

Bonnin and Morris
*p.202, p.203 (Copyright The
Museum of Fine Arts, Houston,
Texas and www.bridgeman art.com)*

Brightwells Fine Art
Fine Art Saleroom,
Easters Court, Leominster,
Herefordshire HR6 0DE
p.141tl

Cheffins
Clifton House, 1&2 Clifton
Road,
Cambridge CB1 7EA
p.47tl, p.111bl, p.213, p.215br

Clevedon Salerooms
The Auction Centre, Kenn
Road, Kenn, Clevedon, Bristol,
BS21 6TT
p.24tr

Dorotheum
Dorotheergasse 17, Vienna,
Austria
www.dorotheum.com
*p.8, p.31bl, p.33, p.36, p.37cr,
p.39tr, p.39br, p.43bl, p.44,
p.45br, p.45tr, p.46, p.47tr, p.48,
p.49tr, p.49bl, p.49br, p.53tl,
p.54, p.60, p.62, p.63bl, p.65bl,
p.67bl, p.69bl, p.70, p.71bl, p.71tr,
p.80, p.81tr, p.82tl, p.83tr, p.83bl,
p.105bl*

Dreweatts
Donnington Priory Salerooms,
Donnington,
Newbury RG14 2JE
www.dnfa.com/donnington
*p.11tl, p.68tl, p.68tr, p.69br,
p.93bl, p.97tr, p.99tl, p.101tr,
p.109bc, p.125tc p.139tl, p.147bl,
p.159tr, p.161tr, p.174, p.217bc,
p.163bl, p.189br*

Jill Fenichell Inc.
169 Prospect Place
Brooklyn NY 11238
www.jillfenichellinc.com
*p.53bl, p.187tl, p.200, p.201,
p.211bl*

Auktionhaus Dr Fischer
Trappensee-Schößchen,
D-74074 Heilbronn Germany
p.117tr

Freeman's
1808 Chestnut Street,
Philadelphia, PA 19103 USA
*p.11r, p.12bl, p.41tl, p.50, p.51br,
p.93tr, p.103tl, p.107bl, p.108l,
p.204, p.205bl, p.206tl, p.206br,
p.209bl, p.209br, p.212*

Gorringes
15 North Street,
Lewes,
East Sussex BN7 2PD
www.gorringes.co.uk
*p.18tl, p.43tr, p.76, p.107cr,
p.143tc, p.51tl, p.51bl, p.135br,
p.215bl*